The Athelings
Or The Three Gifts
Vol. 1

by

Margaret Oliphant

The Athelings
Or The Three Gifts
Vol. 1
by Margaret Oliphant

Copyright © 2023

All Rights reserved.

No part of this publication may be reproduced, stored in a retrieval system, or transmitted in any form or by any means, electronic, mechanical, photocopying or Otherwise, without the written permission of the publisher.
The author/editor asserts the moral right to be identified as the author/editor of this work.

ISBN: 978-93-59957-10-4

Published by

DOUBLE 9 BOOKS

2/13-B, Ansari Road
Daryaganj, New Delhi – 110002
info@double9books.com
www.double9books.com
Tel. 011-40042856

This book is under public domain

ABOUT THE AUTHOR

Margaret Oliphant Wilson Oliphant was a Scottish author and historical writer who usually wrote under the name Mrs. Oliphant. She was born Margaret Oliphant Wilson on April 4, 1828, and died on June 20, 1897. She writes "domestic realism, the historical novel, and tales of the supernatural" as her short stories. Margaret Oliphant was born in Wallyford, near Musselburgh, East Lothian. She was the only daughter and youngest child still living of Margaret Oliphant (c. 1789-17 September 1854) and Francis W. Wilson, a clerk. We lived in Lasswade, Glasgow, and Liverpool when she was a child. In Wallyford, a street called Oliphant Gardens is named after her. As a girl, she was always trying new things with writing. Passages in the Life of Mrs. Margaret Maitland, her first book, came out in 1849. This was about the mostly successful Scottish Free Church movement, which was something her folks agreed with. Next came Caleb Field in 1851, the same year she met publisher William Blackwood in Edinburgh and was asked to write for Blackwood's Magazine. She did so for the rest of her life and wrote over 100 articles, including one that criticized Arthur Dimmesdale in Nathaniel Hawthorne's "The Scarlet Letter."

CONTENTS

BOOK I

CHAPTER I
IN THE STREET

One of them is very pretty—you can see that at a glance: under the simple bonnet, and through the thin little veil, which throws no cloud upon its beauty, shines the sweetest girl's face imaginable. It is only eighteen years old, and not at all of the heroical cast, but it brightens like a passing sunbeam through all the sombre line of passengers, and along the dull background of this ordinary street. There is no resisting that sweet unconscious influence: people smile when they pass her, unawares; it is a natural homage paid involuntarily to the young, sweet, innocent loveliness, unconscious of its own power. People have smiled upon her all her days; she thinks it is because everybody is amiable, and seeks no further for a cause.

The other one is not very pretty; she is twenty: she is taller, paler, not so bright of natural expression, yet as far from being commonplace as can be conceived. They are dressed entirely alike, thriftily dressed in brown merino, with little cloaks exact to the same pattern, and bonnets, of which every bow of ribbon outside, and every little pink rosebud within, is a complete fac-simile of its sister bud and bow. They have little paper-parcels in their hands each of them; they are about the same height, and not much different in age; and to see these twin figures, so entirely resembling each other, passing along at the same inconsistent youthful pace, now rapid and now lingering, you would scarcely be prepared for the characteristic difference in their looks and in their minds.

It is a spring afternoon, cheery but cold, and lamps and shop-windows are already beginning to shine through the ruddy twilight. This is a suburban street, with shops here and there, and sombre lines of houses between. The houses are all graced with "front gardens," strips of ground enriched with a few smoky evergreens, and flower-plots ignorant of flowers; and the shops are of a highly miscellaneous character, adapted to the wants of the locality.

Vast London roars and travails far away to the west and to the south. This is Islington, a mercantile and clerkish suburb. The people on the omnibuses—and all the omnibuses are top-heavy with outside passengers—are people from the City; and at this time in the afternoon, as a general principle, everybody is going home.

The two sisters, by a common consent, come to a sudden pause: it is before a toy-shop; and it is easy to discover by the discussion which follows that there are certain smaller people who form an important part of the household at home.

"Take this, Agnes," says the beautiful sister; "see how pretty! and they could both play with this; but only Bell would care for the doll."

"It is Bell's turn," said Agnes; "Beau had the last one. This we could dress ourselves, for I know mamma has a piece over of their last new frocks. The blue eyes are the best. Stand at the door, Marian, and look for my father, till I buy it; but tell me first which they will like best."

This was not an easy question. The sisters made a long and anxious survey of the window, varied by occasional glances behind them "to see if papa was coming," and concluded by a rapid decision on Agnes's part in favour of one of the ugliest of the dolls. But still Papa did not come; and the girls were proceeding on their way with the doll, a soft and shapeless parcel, added to their former burdens, when a rapid step came up behind them, and a clumsy boy plunged upon the shoulder of the elder.

"Oh, Charlie!" exclaimed Agnes in an aggrieved but undoubting tone. She did not need to look round. This big young brother was unmistakable in his salutations.

"I say, my father's past," said Charlie. "Won't he be pleased to find you two girls out? What do you wander about so late for? it's getting dark. I call that foolish, when you might be out, if you pleased, all the day."

"My boy, you do not know anything about it," said the elder sister with dignity; "and you shall go by yourself if you do not walk quietly. There! people are looking at us; they never looked at us till you came."

"Charlie is so handsome," said Marian laughing, as they all turned a corner, and, emancipated from the public observation, ran along the quiet street, a straggling group, one now pressing before, and now lagging behind. This big boy, however, so far from being handsome, was strikingly the opposite. He had large, loose, ill-compacted limbs, like most young animals of a large growth, and a face which might be called clever, powerful, or good-humoured, but certainly was, without any dispute, ugly. He was of dark complexion, had natural furrows in his brow, and a mouth, wide with fun and happy temper at the present moment, which could close with indomitable obstinacy when occasion served. No fashion could have made Charlie Atheling fashionable; but his plain apparel looked so much plainer and coarser than his sisters', that it had neither neatness nor grace to redeem its homeliness. He was seventeen, tall, *big*, and somewhat clumsy, as unlike as possible to the girls, who had a degree of natural and simple gracefulness not very common in their sphere. Charlie's masculine development was unequivocal; he was a thorough *boy* now, and would be a manful man.

"Charlie, boy, have you been thinking?" asked Agnes suddenly, as the three once more relapsed into a sober pace, and pursued their homeward way together. There was the faintest quiver of ridicule in the elder sister's voice, and Marian looked up for the answer with a smile. The young gentleman gave some portentous hitches of his broad shoulders, twisted his brow into ominous puckers, set his teeth—and at last burst out with indignation and unrestrained vehemence—

"Have I been thinking?—to be sure! but I can't make anything of it, if I think for ever."

"You are worse than a woman, Charlie," said the pretty Marian; "you never can make up your mind."

"Stuff!" cried the big boy loudly; "it isn't making up my mind, it's thinking what will do. You girls know nothing about it. I can't see that one thing's better than another, for my part. One man succeeds and another man's a failure, and yet the one's as good a fellow and as clever to work as the other. I don't know what it means."

"So I suppose you will end with being misanthropical and doing nothing," said Agnes; "and all Charlie Atheling's big intentions will burst, like Beau's soap-bubbles. I would not have that."

"I won't have that, and so you know very well," said Charlie, who was by no means indisposed for a quarrel. "You are always aggravating, you girls—as if you knew anything about it! I'll tell you what; I don't mind how it is, but I'm a man to be something, as sure as I live."

"You are not a man at all, poor little Charlie—you are only a boy," said Marian.

"And we are none of us so sure to live that we should swear by it," said Agnes. "If you are to be something, you should speak better sense than that."

"Oh, a nice pair of tutors you are!" cried Master Charlie. "I'm bigger than the two of you put together—and I'm a man. You may be as envious as you like, but you cannot alter that."

Now, though the girls laughed, and with great contempt scouted the idea of being envious, it is not to be denied that some small morsel of envy concerning masculine privileges lay in the elder sister's heart. It was said at home that Agnes was clever—this was her distinction in the family; and Agnes, having a far-away perception of the fact, greatly longed for some share of those wonderful imaginary advantages which "opened all the world," as she herself said, to a man's ambition; she coloured a little with involuntary excitement, while Marian's sweet and merry laughter still rang in her ear. Marian could afford to laugh—for this beautiful child was neither clever nor ambitious, and had, in all circumstances, the sweetest faculty of content.

"Well, Charlie, a man can do anything," said Agnes; "*we* are obliged to put up with trifles. If I were a man, I should be content with nothing less than the greatest—I know that!"

"Stuff!" answered the big boy once more; "you may romance about it as you like, but I know better. Who is to care whether you are content or not? You must be only what you can, if you were the greatest hero in the world."

"I do not know, for my part, what you are talking of," said Marian. "Is this all about what you are going to do, Charlie, and because you cannot make up your mind whether you will be a clerk in papa's office, or go to old Mr Foggo's to learn to be a lawyer? I don't see what heroes have to do with it either one way or other. You ought to go to your business quietly, and be content. Why should *you* be better than papa?"

The question was unanswerable. Charlie hitched his great shoulders, and made marvellous faces, but replied nothing. Agnes went on steadily in a temporary abstraction; Marian ran on in advance. The street was only half-built—one of those quietest of surburban streets which are to be found only in the outskirts of great towns. The solitary little houses, some quite apart, some in pairs—detached and semi-detached, according to the proper description—stood in genteel retirement within low walls and miniature shrubberies. There was nothing ever to be seen in this stillest of inhabited places—therefore it was called Bellevue: and the inhabitants veiled their parlour windows behind walls and boarded railings, lest their privacy should be invaded by the vulgar vision of butcher, or baker, or greengrocer's boy. Other eyes than those of the aforesaid professional people never disturbed the composure of Laurel Cottage and Myrtle Cottage, Elmtree Lodge and Halcyon House—wherefore the last new house had a higher wall and a closer railing than any of its predecessors; and it was edifying to observe everybody's virtuous resolution to see nothing where there was visibly nothing to see.

At the end of this closed-up and secluded place, one light, shining from an unshuttered window, made a gleam of cheerfulness through the respectable gloom. Here you could see shadows large and small moving upon the white blind—could see the candles shifted about, and the sudden reddening of the stirred fire. A wayfarer, when by chance there was one, could scarcely fail to pause with a momentary sentiment of neighbourship and kindness opposite this shining window. It was the only evidence in the darkness of warm and busy human life. This was the home of the three young Athelings—as yet the centre and boundary of all their pleasures, and almost all their desires.

CHAPTER II
HOME

The house is old for this locality—larger than this family could have afforded, had it been in better condition,—a cheap house out of repair. It is impossible to see what is the condition of the little garden before the door; but the bushes are somewhat straggling, and wave their long arms about in the rising wind. There is a window on either side of the door, and the house is but two stories high: it is the most commonplace of houses, perfectly comfortable and uninteresting, so far as one may judge from without. Inside, the little hall is merely a passage, with a door on either side, a long row of pegs fastened against the wall, and a strip of brightly-painted oil-cloth on the floor. The parlour door is open—there are but two candles, yet the place is bright; and in it is the lighted window which shines so cheerily into the silent street. The father sits by the fire in the only easy-chair which this apartment boasts; the mother moves about on sundry nameless errands, of which she herself could scarcely give a just explanation; yet somehow that comfortable figure passing in and out through light and shadow adds an additional charm to the warmth and comfort of the place. Two little children are playing on the rug before the fire—very little children, twins scarcely two years old—one of them caressing the slippered foot of Mr Atheling, the other seated upon a great paper book full of little pictures, which serves at once as amusement for the little mind, and repose for the chubby little frame. They are rosy, ruddy, merry imps, as ever brightened a fireside; and it is hard to believe they are of the same family as Charlie and Agnes and Marian. For there is a woeful gap between the elder and the younger children of this house—an interval of heavy, tardy, melancholy years, the records of which are written, many names, upon one gravestone, and upon the hearts of these two cheerful people, among their children at their own hearth. They have lived through their day of visitation, and come again into the light beyond; but it is easy to understand the peculiar tenderness with which father and mother bend over these last little children—angels of consolation—and how everything in the house yields to the pretty childish caprice of little Bell and little Beau.

Yes, of course, you have found it out: everybody finds it out at the first glance; everybody returns to it with unfailing criticism. To tell the truth, the house is a very cheap house, being so large a one. Had it been in good order, the Athelings could never have pretended to such a "desirable family residence" as this house in Bellevue; and so you perceive this room has been papered by Charlie and the girls and Mrs Atheling. It is a very pretty paper, and was a great bargain; but unfortunately it is not matched—one-half of the pattern, in two or three places, is hopelessly divorced from the other half. They were very zealous, these amateur workpeople, but they were not born paperhangers, and, with the best intentions in the world, have drawn the walls awry. At the time Mrs Atheling was extremely mortified, and Agnes overcome with humiliation; but Charlie and Marian thought it very good fun; Papa burst into shouts of laughter; Bell and Beau chorused lustily, and at length even the unfortunate managers of the work forgave themselves. It never was altered, because a new paper is an important consideration where so many new frocks, coats, and bonnets are perpetually wanting: everybody became accustomed to it; it was an unfailing source of family witticism; and Mrs Atheling came to find so much relaxation from her other cares in the constant mental effort to piece together the disjointed pattern, that even to her there was consolation in this dire and lamentable failure. Few strangers came into the family-room, but every visitor who by chance entered it, with true human perversity turned his eyes from the comfort and neatness of the apartment, and from the bright faces of its occupants, to note the flowers and arabesques of the pretty paper, wandering all astray over this unfortunate wall.

Yet it was a pretty scene—with Marian's beautiful face at one side of the table, and the bright intelligence of Agnes at the other—the rosy children on the rug, the father reposing from his day's labour, the mother busy with her sweet familiar never-ending cares; even Charlie, ugly and characteristic, added to the family completeness. The head of the house was only a clerk in a merchant's office, with a modest stipend of two hundred pounds a-year. All the necessities of the family, young and old, had to be supplied out of this humble income. You may suppose there was not much over, and that the household chancellor of the exchequer had enough to do, even when assisted by that standing committee with which she consulted solemnly over every little outlay. The committee was prudent, but it was not infallible. Agnes, the leading member, had extravagant notions. Marian, more careful, had still a weakness for ribbons and household embellishments, bright and clean and new. Sometimes the committee *en permanence* was abruptly dismissed by its indignant president, charged with revolutionary sentiments, and a total ignorance of sound financial principles. Now and then there occurred a monetary crisis. On the whole, however, the domestic kingdom was wisely governed, and the seven Athelings, parents and children, lived and prospered, found it possible to have even holiday dresses, and books from the circulating library, ribbons for the girls, and toys for the babies, out of their two hundred pounds a-year.

Tea was on the table; yet the first thing to be done was to open out the little paper parcels, which proved to contain enclosures no less important than those very ribbons, which the finance committee had this morning decided upon as indispensable. Mrs Atheling unrolled them carefully, and held them out to the light. She shook her head; they had undertaken this serious responsibility all by themselves, these rash imprudent girls.

"Now, mamma, what do you think? I told you we could choose them; and the man said they were half as dear again six months ago," cried the triumphant Marian.

Again Mrs Atheling shook her head. "My dears," said the careful mother, "how do you think such a colour as this can last till June?"

This solemn question somewhat appalled the youthful purchasers. "It is a very pretty colour, mamma," said Agnes, doubtfully.

"So it is," said the candid critic; "but you know it will fade directly. I always told you so. It is only fit for people who have a dozen bonnets, and can afford to change them. I am quite surprised at you, girls; you ought to have known a great deal better. Of course the colour will fly directly: the first sunny day will make an end of that. But *I* cannot help it, you know; and, faded or not faded, it must do till June."

The girls exchanged glances of discomfiture. "Till June!" said Agnes; "and it is only March now. Well, one never knows what may happen before June."

This was but indifferent consolation, but it brought Charlie to the table to twist the unfortunate ribbon, and let loose his opinion. "They ought to wear wide-awakes. That's what they ought to have," said Charlie. "Who cares for all that trumpery? not old Foggo, I'm sure, nor Miss Willsie; and they are all the people we ever see."

"Hold your peace, Charlie," said Mrs Atheling, "and don't say old Foggo, you rude boy. He is the best friend you have, and a real gentleman; and what would your papa do with such a set of children about him, if Mr Foggo did not drop in now and then for some sensible conversation. It will be a long time before you try to make yourself company for papa."

"Foggo is not so philanthropical, Mary," said Papa, for the first time interposing; "he has an eye to something else than sensible conversation. However, be quiet and sit down, you set of children, and let us have some tea."

The ribbons accordingly were lifted away, and placed in a heap upon a much-used work-table which stood in the window. The kettle sang by the fire. The tea was made. Into two small chairs of wickerwork, raised upon high stilts to reach the table, were hoisted Bell and Beau. The talk of these small interlocutors had all this time been incessant, but untranslatable. It was the unanimous opinion of the family Atheling that you could "make out every word" spoken by these little personages, and that they were quite remarkable in their intelligibility; yet there were difficulties in the way, and everybody had not leisure for the close study of this peculiar language, nor the abstract attention necessary for a proper comprehension of all its happy sayings. So Bell and Beau, to the general public, were but a merry little chorus to the family drama, interrupting nothing, and being interrupted by nobody. Like crickets and singing-birds, and all musical creatures, their happy din grew louder as the conversation rose; but there was not one member of this loving circle who objected to have his voice drowned in the jubilant uproar of those sweet small voices, the unceasing music of this happy house.

After tea, it was Marian's "turn," as it appeared, to put the little orchestra to bed. It was well for the little cheeks that they were made of a more elastic material than those saintly shrines and reliquaries which pious pilgrims wore away with kissing; and Charlie, mounting one upon each shoulder, carried the small couple up-stairs. It was touching to see the universal submission to these infants: the house had been very sad before they came, and these twin blossoms had ushered into a second summer the bereaved and heavy household life.

When Bell and Beau were satisfactorily asleep and disposed of, Mrs Atheling sat down to her sewing, as is the wont of exemplary mothers. Papa found his occupation in a newspaper, from which now and then he read a scrap of news aloud. Charlie, busy about some solitary study, built himself round with books at a side-table. Agnes and Marian, with great zeal and some excitement, laid their heads together over the trimming of their bonnets. The ribbon was very pretty, though it was unprofitable; perhaps in their secret hearts these girls liked it the better for its unthrifty delicacy, but they were too "well brought up" to own to any such perverse feeling. At any rate, they were very much concerned about their pretty occupation, and tried a hundred different fashions before they decided upon the plainest and oldest fashion of all. They had taste enough to make their plain little straw-bonnets very pretty to look at, but were no more skilled in millinery than in paperhanging, and timid of venturing upon anything new. The night flew on to all of them in these quiet businesses; and Time went more heavily through many a festive and courtly place than he did through this little parlour, where there was no attempt at pleasure-making. When the bonnets were finished, it had grown late. Mr Foggo had not come this night for any sensible conversation; neither had Agnes been tempted to join Charlie at the side-table, where lay a miscellaneous collection of papers, packed within an overflowing blotting-book, her indisputable property. Agnes had other ambition than concerned the trimming of bonnets, and had spoiled more paper in her day than the paper of this parlour wall; but we pause till the morning to exhibit the gift of Agnes Atheling, how it was regarded, and what it was.

CHAPTER III
AGNES

Dearest friend! most courteous reader! suspend your judgment. It was not her fault. This poor child had no more blame in the matter than Marian had for her beauty, which was equally involuntary. Agnes Atheling was not wise; she had no particular gift for conversation, and none whatever for logic; no accomplishments, and not a very great deal of information. To tell the truth, while it was easy enough to discover what she had not, it was somewhat difficult to make out precisely what she had to distinguish her from other people. She was a good girl, but by no means a model one; full of impatiences, resentments, and despairs now and then, as well as of hopes, jubilant and glorious, and a vague but grand ambition. She herself knew herself quite as little as anybody else did; for consciousness of power and prescience of fame, if these are signs of genius, did not belong to Agnes. Yet genius, in some kind and degree, certainly did belong to her, for the girl had that strange faculty of expression which is as independent of education, knowledge, or culture as any wandering angel. When she had anything to say (upon paper), she said it with so much grace and beauty of language, that Mr Atheling's old correspondents puzzled and shook their grey heads over it, charmed and astonished without knowing why, and afterwards declared to each other that Atheling must be a clever fellow, though they had never discovered it before; and a clever fellow he must have been indeed, could he have clothed these plain sober sentiments of his in such a radiant investiture of fancy and youth. For Agnes was the letter-writer of the household, and in her young sincerity, and with her visionary delight in all things beautiful, was not content to make a dutiful inquiry, on her mother's part, for an old ailing country aunt, or to convey a bit of city gossip to some clerkish contemporary of her father's, without induing the humdrum subject with such a glow and glory of expression that the original proprietors of the sentiment scarcely knew it in its dazzling gear. She had been letting her pearls and her diamonds drop from her lips after this fashion, with the prodigality of a young spendthrift—only astonishing the respectable people who were on letter-writing terms with Mr and Mrs Atheling—for two or three years past. But time only strengthened the natural bent of this young creature, to whom Providence had given, almost her sole dower, that gift of speech which is so often withheld from those who have the fullest and highest opportunity for its exercise. Agnes, poor girl! young, inexperienced, and uninstructed, had not much wisdom to communicate to the world—not much of anything, indeed, save the vague and splendid dreams—the variable, impossible, and inconsistent speculations of youth; but she had the gift, and with the gift she had the sweet spontaneous impulse which made it a delight. They were proud of her at home. Mr and Mrs Atheling, with the tenderest exultation, rejoiced over Marian, who was pretty, and Agnes, who was clever; yet, loving these two still more than they admired them, they by no means realised the fact that the one had beauty and the other genius of a rare and unusual kind. We are even obliged to confess that at times their mother had compunctions, and doubted whether Agnes, a poor man's daughter, and like to be a poor man's wife, ought to be permitted so much time over that overflowing blotting-book. Mrs Atheling, when her own ambition and pride in her child did not move her otherwise, pondered much whether it would not be wiser to teach the girls dress-making or some other practical occupation, "for they may not marry; and if anything should happen to William or me!—as of course we are growing old, and will not live for ever," she said to herself in her tender and anxious heart. But the girls had not yet learned dress-making, in spite of Mrs Atheling's fears; and though Marian could "cut out" as well as her mother, and Agnes, more humble, worked with her needle to the universal admiration, no speculations as to "setting them up in business" had entered the parental brain. So Agnes continued at the side-table, sometimes writing very rapidly and badly, sometimes copying out with the most elaborate care and delicacy—copying out even a second time, if by accident or misfortune a single blot came upon the well-beloved page. This occupation alternated with all manner of domestic occupations. The young writer was as far from being an abstracted personage as it is possible to conceive; and from the momentous matter of the household finances to the dressing of the doll, and the childish play of Bell and Beau, nothing came amiss to the incipient author. With this sweet stream of common life around her, you may be sure her genius did her very little harm.

And when all the domestic affairs were over—when Mr Atheling had finished his newspaper, and Mrs Atheling put aside her work-basket, and Mr Foggo was out of the way—then Papa was wont to look over his shoulder to his eldest child. "You may read some of your nonsense, if you like, Agnes," said the household head; and it was Agnes's custom upon this invitation, though not without a due degree of coyness, to gather up her papers, draw her chair into the corner, and read what she had written. Before Agnes began, Mrs Atheling invariably stretched out her hand for her work-basket, and was invariably rebuked by her husband; but Marian's white hands rustled on unreproved, and Charlie sat still at his grammar. It was popularly reported in the family that Charlie kept on steadily learning his verbs even while he listened to Agnes's story. He said so himself, who was the best authority; but we by no means pledge ourselves to the truth of the statement.

And so the young romance was read: there was some criticism, but more approval; and in reality none of them knew what to think of it, any more than the youthful author did. They were too closely concerned to be cool judges, and, full of interest and admiration as they were, could not quite overcome the oddness and novelty of the idea that "our Agnes" might possibly one day be famous, and write for the world. Mr Atheling himself, who was most inclined to be critical, had the strangest confusion of feelings upon this subject, marvelling much within himself whether "the child" really had this singular endowment, or if it was only their own partial judgment which magnified her powers. The family father could come to no satisfactory conclusion upon the subject, but still smiled at himself, and wondered, when his daughter's story brought tears to his eyes, or sympathy or indignation to his heart. It moved *him* without dispute,—it moved Mamma there, hastily rubbing out the moisture from the corner of her eyes. Even Charlie was disturbed over his grammar. "Yes," said Mr Atheling, "but then you see she belongs to us; and though all this certainly never could have come into *my* head, yet it is natural I should sympathise with it; but it is a very different thing when you think of the world."

So it was, as different a thing as possible; for the world had no anxious love to sharpen *its* criticism—did not care a straw whether the young writer was eloquent or nonsensical; and just in proportion to its indifference was like to be the leniency of its judgment. These good people did not think of that; they made wonderful account of their own partiality, but never reckoned upon that hypercritical eye of love which will not be content with a questionable excellence; and so they pondered and marvelled with an excitement half amusing and half solemn. What would other people think?—what would be the judgment of the world?

As for Agnes, she was as much amused as the rest at the thought of being "an author," and laughed, with her bright eyes running over, at this grand anticipation; for she was too young and too inexperienced to see more than a delightful novelty and unusualness in her possible fame. In the mean time she was more interested in what she was about than in the result of it, and pleased herself with the turn of her pretty sentences, and the admirable orderliness of her manuscript; for she was only a girl.

CHAPTER IV
MARIAN

Marian Atheling had as little choice in respect to her particular endowment as her sister had; less, indeed, for it cost her nothing—not an hour's thought or a moment's exertion. She could not help shining forth so fair and sweet upon the sober background of this family life; she could not help charming every stranger who looked into her sweet eyes. She was of no particular "style" of beauty, so far as we are aware; she was even of no distinct complexion of loveliness, but wavered with the sweetest shade of uncertainty between dark and fair, tall and little. For hers was not the beauty of genius—it was not exalted and heroical expression—it was not tragic force or eloquence of features; it was something less distinct and more subtle even than these. Hair that caught the sunshine, and brightened under its glow; eyes which laughed a sweet response of light before the fair eyelids fell over them in that sweet inconsistent mingling of frankness and shyness which is the very charm of girlhood; cheeks as soft and bloomy and fragrant as any flower,—these seemed but the appropriate language in which alone this innocent, radiant, beautiful youth could find fit expression. For beauty of expression belonged to Marian as well as more obvious beauties; there was an entire sweet harmony between the language and the sentiment of nature upon this occasion. The face would have been beautiful still, had its possessor been a fool or discontented; as it was, being only the lovely exponent of a heart as pure, happy, and serene as heart could be, the face was perfect. Criticism had nothing to do with an effect so sudden and magical: this young face shone and brightened like a sunbeam, touching the hearts of those it beamed upon. Mere admiration was scarcely the sentiment with which people looked at her; it was pure tenderness, pleasure, unexpected delight, which made the chance passengers in the street smile as they passed her by. Their hearts warmed to this fair thing of God's making—they "blessed her unaware." Eighteen years old, and possessed of this rare gift, Marian still did not know what rude admiration was, though she went out day by day alone and undefended, and would not have faltered at going anywhere, if her mother bade or necessity called. *She* knew nothing of those stares and impertinent annoyances which fastidious ladies sometimes complained of, and of which she had read in books. Marian asserted roundly, and with unhesitating confidence, that "it was complete nonsense"—"it was not true;" and went upon her mother's errands through all the Islingtonian streets as safely as any heroine ever went through ambuscades and prisons. She believed in lovers and knights of romance vaguely, but fervently,—believed even, we confess, in the melodramatic men who carry off fair ladies, and also in disguised princes and Lords of Burleigh; but knew nothing whatever, in her own most innocent and limited experience, of any love but the love of home. And Marian had heard of bad men and bad women,—nay, *knew*, in Agnes's story, the most impossible and short-sighted of villains—a true rascal of romance, whose snares were made on purpose for discovery,—but had no more fear of such than she had of lions or tigers, the Gunpowder Plot, or the Spanish Inquisition. Safe as among her lawful vassals, this young girl went and came—safe as in a citadel, dwelt in her father's house, untempted, untroubled, in the most complete and thorough security. So far as she had come upon the sunny and flowery way of her young life, her beauty had been no gift of peril to Marian, and she had no fear of what was to come.

And no one is to suppose that Mrs Atheling's small means were strained to do honour to, or "set off," her pretty daughter. These good people, though they loved much to see their children happy and well esteemed, had no idea of any such unnecessary efforts; and Marian shone out of her brown merino frock, and her little pink rosebuds, as sweetly as ever shone a princess in the purple and pall of her high estate. Mrs Atheling thought Marian "would look well in anything," in the pride of her heart, as she pinched the bit of white lace round Marian's neck when Mr Foggo and Miss Willsie were coming to tea. It was indeed the general opinion of the household, and that other people shared it was sufficiently proved by the fact that Miss Willsie herself begged for a pattern of that very little collar, which was so becoming. Marian gave the pattern with the greatest alacrity, yet protested that Miss Willsie had many collars a great deal prettier—which indeed was very true.

And Marian was her mother's zealous assistant in all household occupations—not more willing, but with more execution and practical power than Agnes, who, by dint of a hasty anxiety for perfection, made an intolerable amount of blunders. Marian was more matter-of-fact, and knew better what she could do; she was constantly busy, morning and night, keeping always in hand some morsel of fancy-work, with which to occupy herself at irregular times after the ordinary work was over. Agnes also had bits of fancy-work in hand; but the difference herein between the two sisters was this, that Marian finished *her* pretty things, while Agnes's uncompleted enterprises were always turning up in some old drawer or work-table, and were never brought to a conclusion. Marian made collars for her mother, frills for Bell and Beau, and a very fine purse for Charlie; which Charlie, having nothing to put in the same, rejected disdainfully: but it was a very rare thing indeed for Agnes to come to an end of any such labour. With Marian, too, lay the honour of far superior accuracy and precision in the important particular of "cutting out." These differences furthered the appropriate division of labour, and the household work made happy progress under their united hands.

To this we have only to add, that Marian Atheling was merry without being witty, and intelligent without being clever. She, too, was a good girl; but she also had her faults: she was sometimes saucy, very often self-willed, yet had fortunately thus far shown a sensible perception of cases which were beyond her own power of settling. She had the greatest interest in Agnes's story-telling, but was extremely impatient to know the end before the beginning, which the hapless young author was not always in circumstances to tell; and Marian made countless suggestions, interfering arbitrarily and vexatiously with the providence of fiction, and desiring all sorts of impossible rewards and punishments. But Marian's was no quiet or superficial criticism: how she burned with indignation at that poor unbelievable villain!—how she triumphed when all the good people put him down!—with what entire and fervid interest she entered into everybody's fortune! It was worth while being present at one of these family readings, if only to see the flutter and tumult of sympathies which greeted the tale.

And we will not deny that Marian had possibly a far-off idea that she was pretty—an idea just so indistinct and distant as to cause a momentary blush and sparkle—a momentary flutter, half of pleasure and half of shame, when it chanced to glide across her young unburdened heart; but of her beauty and its influence this innocent girl had honestly no conception. Everybody smiled upon her everywhere. Even Mr Foggo's grave and saturnine countenance slowly brightened when her sweet face shone upon him. Marian did not suppose that these smiles had anything to do with her; she went upon her way with a joyous young belief in the goodness of everybody, except the aforesaid impossible people, who were unspeakably black, beyond anything that ever was painted, to the simple imagination of Marian. She had no great principle of abstract benevolence to make her charitable; she was strongly in favour of the instant and overwhelming punishment of all these imaginary criminals; but for the rest of the world, Marian looked them all in the face, frank and shy and sweet, with her beautiful eyes. She was content to offer that small right hand of kindliest fellowship, guileless and unsuspecting, to them all.

CHAPTER V
CHARLIE

This big boy was about as far from being handsome as any ordinary imagination could conceive: his large loose limbs, his big features, his swarthy complexion, though they were rather uglier in their present development than they were likely to be when their possessor was full-grown and a man, could never, by any chance, gain him the moderate credit of good looks. He was not handsome emphatically, and yet there never was a more expressive face: that great furrowed brow of his went up in ripples and waves of laughter when the young gentleman was so minded, and descended in rolls of cloud when there was occasion for such a change. His mouth was not a pretty mouth: the soft curve of Cupid's bow, the proud Napoleonic curl, were as different as you could suppose from the indomitable and graceless upper-lip of Charlie Atheling. Yet when that obstinate feature came down in fixed and steady impenetrability, a more emphatic expression never sat on the haughtiest curve of Greece. He was a tolerably good boy, but he had his foible. Charlie, we are grieved to say, was obstinate—marvellously obstinate, unpersuadable, and beyond the reach of reasoning. If anything could have made this propensity justifiable—as nothing could possibly make it more provoking—it was, that the big boy was very often in the right. Time after time, by force of circumstances, everybody else was driven to give in to him: whether it really was by means of astute and secret calculation of all the chances of the question, nobody could tell; but every one knew how often Charlie's opinion was confirmed by the course of events, and how very seldom his odd penetration was deceived. This, as a natural consequence, made everybody very hot and very resentful who happened to disagree with Charlie, and caused a great amount of jubilation and triumph in the house on those occasions, unfrequent as they were, when his boyish infallibility was proved in the wrong.

Yet Charlie was not clever. The household could come to no satisfactory conclusion upon this subject. He did not get on with his moderate studies either quicker or better than any ordinary boy of his years. He had no special turn for literature either, though he did not disdain *Peter Simple* and *Midshipman Easy*. These renowned productions of genius held the highest place at present in that remote corner of Charlie's interest which was reserved for the fine arts; but we are obliged to confess that this big boy had wonderfully bad taste in general, and could not at all appreciate the higher excellences of art. Besides all this, no inducement whatever could tempt Charlie to the writing of the briefest letter, or to any exercise of his powers of composition, if any such powers belonged to him. No, he could not be clever — and yet — —

They did not quite like to give up the question, the mother and sisters. They indulged in the loftiest flights of ambition for him, as heaven-aspiring, and built on as slender a foundation, as any bean-stalk of romance. They endeavoured greatly, with much anxiety and care, to make him clever, and to make him ambitious, after their own model; but this obstinate and self-willed individual was not to be coerced. So far as this matter went, Charlie had a certain affectionate contempt for them all, with their feminine fancies and imaginations. He said only "Stuff!" when he listened to the grand projects of the girls, and to Agnes's flush of enthusiastic confidence touching that whole unconquered world which was open to "a man!" Charlie hitched his great shoulders, frowned down upon her with all the furrows of his brow, laughed aloud, and went off to his grammar. This same grammar he worked at with his usual obstinate steadiness. He had not a morsel of liking for "his studies;" but he "went in" at them doggedly, just as he might have broken stones or hewed wood, had that been a needful process. Nobody ever does know the secret of anybody else's character till life and time have evolved the same; so it is not wonderful that these good people were a little puzzled about Charlie, and did not quite know how to dispose of their obstinate big boy.

Charlie himself, however, we are glad to say, was sometimes moved to take his sisters into his confidence. *They* knew that some ambition did stir within that Titanic boyish frame. They were in the secret of the great discussion which was at present going on in the breast of Charlie, whose whole thoughts, to tell the truth, were employed about the momentous question — What he was to be? There was not a very wide choice in his power. He was not seduced by the red coat and the black coat, like the ass of the problem. The syrens of wealth and fame did not sing in his ears, to tempt him to one course or another. He had two homely possibilities before him — a this, and a that. He had a stout intention to be *something*, and no such ignoble sentiment as content found place in Charlie's heart; wherefore long, animated, and doubtful was the self-controversy. Do not smile, good youth, at Charlie's two chances — they are small in comparison of yours, but they were the only chances visible to him; the one was the merchant's office over which Mr Atheling presided — head clerk, with his two hundred pounds a-year; the other was, grandiloquently—by the girls, not by Charlie—called the law; meaning thereby, however, only the solicitor's office, the lawful empire and domain of Mr Foggo. Between these two legitimate and likely regions for making a fortune, the lad wavered with a most doubtful and inquiring mind. His introduction to each was equally good; for Mr Atheling was confidential and trusted, and Mr Foggo, as a mysterious rumour went, was not only most entirely trusted and confidential, but even in secret a partner in the concern. Wherefore long and painful were the ruminations of Charlie, and marvellous the balance which he made of precedent and example. Let nobody suppose, however, that this question was discussed in idleness. Charlie all this time was actually in the office of Messrs Cash, Ledger, and Co., his father's employers. He was there on a probationary and experimental footing, but he was very far from making up his mind to remain. It was an extremely difficult argument, although carried on solely in the deep invisible caverns of the young aspirant's mind.

The same question, however, was also current in the family, and remained undecided by the household parliament. With much less intense and personal earnestness, "everybody" went over the for and against, and contrasted the different chances. Charlie listened, but made no sign. When he had made up his own mind, the young gentleman proposed to himself to signify his decision publicly, and win over this committee of the whole house to his view of the question. In the mean time he reserved what he had to say; but so far, it is certain that Mr Foggo appeared more tempting than Mr Atheling. The family father had been twenty or thirty years at this business of his, and his income was two hundred pounds—"that would not do for me," said Charlie; whereas Mr Foggo's income, position, and circumstances were alike a mystery, and might be anything. This had considerable influence in the argument, but was not conclusive; for successful merchants were indisputably more numerous than successful lawyers, and Charlie was not aware how high a lawyer who was only an attorney could reach, and had his doubts upon the subject. In the mean time, however, pending the settlement of this momentous question, Charlie worked at two grammars instead of one, and put all his force to his study. Force was the only word which could express the characteristic power of this boy, if even *that* can give a sufficient idea of it. He had no love for his French or for his Latin, yet learned his verbs with a manful obstinacy worthy all honour; and it is not easy to define what was the special gift of Charlie. It was not a describable thing, separate from his character, like beauty or like genius—it *was* his character, intimate and not to be distinguished from himself.

CHAPTER VI
PAPA AND MAMMA

The father of this family, as we have already said, was a clerk in a merchant's office, with a salary of two hundred pounds a-year. He was a man of fifty, with very moderate abilities, but character unimpeachable—a perfect type of his class—steadily marching on in his common routine—doing all his duties without pretension—somewhat given to laying down the law in respect to business—and holding a very grand opinion of the importance of commerce in general, and of the marvellous undertakings of London in particular. Yet this good man was not entirely circumscribed by his "office." He had that native spring of life and healthfulness in him which belongs to those who have been born in, and never have forgotten, the country. The country, most expressive of titles!—he had always kept in his recollection the fragrance of the ploughed soil, the rustle of the growing grass; so, though he lived in Islington, and had his office in the City, he was not a Cockney—a happy and most enviable distinction. His wife, too, was country born and country bred; and two ancestral houses, humble enough, yet standing always among the trees and fields, belonged to the imagination of their children. This was a great matter—for the roses on her grandmother's cottage-wall bloomed perpetually in the fancy of Agnes; and Marian and Charlie knew the wood where Papa once went a-nutting, as well as—though with a more ideal perception than, Papa himself had known it. Even little Bell and Beau knew of a store of secret primroses blooming for ever on a fairy bank, where their mother long ago, in the days of her distant far-off childhood, had seen them blow, and taken them into her heart. Happy primroses, that never faded! for all the children of this house had dreamed and gathered them in handfuls, yet there they were for ever. It was strange how this link of connection with the far-off rural life refined the fancy of these children; it gave them a region of romance, into which they could escape at all times. They did not know its coarser features, and they found refuge in it from the native vulgarity of their own surroundings. Happy effect to all imaginative people, of some ideal and unknown land.

The history of the family was a very common one. Two-and-twenty years ago, William Atheling and Mary Ellis had ventured to marry, having only a very small income, limited prospects, and all the indescribable hopes and chances of youth. Then had come the children, joy, toil, and lamentation—then the way of life had opened up upon them, step by step; and they had fainted, and found it weary, yet, helpless and patient, had toiled on. They never had a chance, these good people, of running away from their fate. If such a desperate thought ever came to them, it must have been dismissed at once, being hopeless; and they stood at their post under the heavy but needful compulsion of ordinary duties, living through many a heartbreak, bearing many a bereavement—voiceless souls, uttering no outcry except to the ear of God. Now they had lived through their day of visitation. God had removed the cloud from their heads and the terror from their heart: their own youth was over, but the youth of their children, full of hopes and possibilities still brighter than their own had been, rejoiced these patient hearts; and the warm little hands of the twin babies, children of their old age, led them along with delight and hopefulness upon their own unwearying way. Such was the family story; it was a story of life, very full, almost overflowing with the greatest and first emotions of humanity, but it was not what people call eventful. The private record, like the family register, brimmed over with those first makings and foundations of history, births and deaths; but few vicissitudes of fortune, little success and little calamity, fell upon the head of the good man whose highest prosperity was this two hundred pounds a-year. And so now they reckoned themselves in very comfortable circumstances, and were disturbed by nothing but hopes and doubts about the prospects of the children—hopes full of brightness present and visible, doubts that were almost as good as hope.

There was but one circumstance of romance in the simple chronicle. Long ago—the children did not exactly know when, or how, or in what manner—Mr Atheling did somebody an extraordinary and mysterious benefit. Papa was sometimes moved to tell them of it in a general way, sheltering himself under vague and wide descriptions. The story was of a young man, handsome, gay, and extravagant, of rank far superior to Mr Atheling's—of how he fell into dissipation, and was tempted to crime—and how at the very crisis "I happened to be in the way, and got hold of him, and showed him the real state of the case; how I heard what he was going to do, and of course would betray him; and how, even if he could do it, it would be certain ruin, disgrace, and misery. That was the whole matter," said Mr

Atheling—and his affectionate audience listened with awe and a mysterious interest, very eager to know something more definite of the whole matter than this concise account of it, yet knowing that all interrogation was vain. It was popularly suspected that Mamma knew the full particulars of this bit of romance, but Mamma was as impervious to questions as the other head of the house. There was also a second fytte to this story, telling how Mr Atheling himself undertook the venture of revealing his hapless hero's misfortunes to the said hero's elder brother, a very grand and exalted personage; how the great man, shocked, and in terror for the family honour, immediately delivered the culprit, and sent him abroad. "Then he offered me money," said Mr Atheling quietly. This was the climax of the tale, at which everybody was expected to be indignant; and very indignant, accordingly, everybody was.

Yet there was a wonderful excitement in the thought that this hero of Papa's adventure was now, as Papa intimated, a man of note in the world— that they themselves unwittingly read his name in the papers sometimes, and that other people spoke of him to Mr Atheling as a public character, little dreaming of the early connection between them. How strange it was!— but no entreaty and no persecution could prevail upon Papa to disclose his name. "Suppose we should meet him some time!" exclaimed Agnes, whose imagination sometimes fired with the thought of reaching that delightful world of society where people always spoke of books, and genius was the highest nobility—a world often met with in novels. "If you did," said Mr Atheling, "it will be all the better for you to know nothing about this," and so the controversy always ended; for in this matter at least, firm as the most scrupulous old knight of romance, Papa stood on his honour.

As for the good and tender mother of this house, she had no story to tell. The girls, it is true, knew about *her* girlish companions very nearly as well as if these, now most sober and middle-aged personages, had been playmates of their own; they knew the names of the pigeons in the old dovecote, the history of the old dog, the number of the apples on the great apple-tree; also they had a kindly recollection of one old lover of Mamma's, concerning whom they were shy to ask further than she was pleased to reveal. But all Mrs Atheling's history was since her marriage: she had been but a young girl with an untouched heart before that grand event, which introduced her, in her own person, to the unquiet ways of life; and her recollections chiefly turned upon the times "when we lived in—— Street,"—"when we took that new house in the terrace,"—"when we came to Bellevue." This Bellevue residence was a great point in the eyes of Mrs Atheling. She herself had always kept her original weakness for gentility, and to live in a street where there was no straight line of commonplace houses, but only villas, detached and semi-detached, and where every house had a name to itself, was no small step in advance—particularly as the house was really cheap, really large, as such houses go, and had only the slight disadvantage of being out of repair. Mrs Atheling lamed her most serviceable finger with attempts at carpentry, and knocked her own knuckles with misdirected hammering, yet succeeded in various shifts that answered very well, and produced that grand *chef-d'œuvre* of paperhanging which made more amusement than any professional decoration ever made, and was just as comfortable. So the good mother was extremely well pleased with her house. She was not above the ambition of calling it either Atheling Lodge, or Hawthorn Cottage, but it was very hard to make a family decision upon the prettiest name; so the house of the Athelings, with its eccentric garden, its active occupants, and its cheery parlour-window, was still only Number Ten, Bellevue.

And there in the summer sunshine, and in the wintry dawning, at eight o'clock, Mr Atheling took his seat at the table, said grace, and breakfasted; from thence at nine to a moment, well brushed and buttoned, the good man went upon his daily warfare to the City. There all the day long the pretty twins played, the mother exercised her careful housewifery, the sweet face of Marian shone like a sunbeam, and the fancies of Agnes wove themselves into separate and real life. All the day long the sun shone in at the parlour window upon a thrifty and well-worn carpet, which all his efforts could not spoil, and dazzled the eyes of Bell and Beau, and troubled the heart of Mamma finding out spots of dust, and suspicions of cobwebs which had escaped her own detection. And when the day was done, and richer people were thinking of dinner, once more, punctual to a moment, came the well-known step on the gravel, and the well-known summons at the door; for at six o'clock Mr Atheling came home to his cheerful tea-table, as contented and respectable a householder, as happy a father, as was in England. And after tea came the newspaper and Mr Foggo; and after Mr Foggo came the readings of Agnes; and so the family said good-night, and slept and rested, to rise again on the next morning to just such another day. Nothing interrupted this happy uniformity; nothing broke in upon the calm and kindly usage of these familiar hours. Mrs Atheling had a mighty deal of thinking to do, by reason of her small income; now and then the girls were obliged to consent to be disappointed of some favourite project of their own—and sometimes even Papa, in a wilful fit of self-denial, refused himself for a few nights his favourite newspaper; but these were but passing shadows upon the general content. Through all these long winter evenings, the one lighted window of this family room brightened the gloomy gentility of Bellevue, and imparted something of heart and kindness to the dull and mossy suburban street. They "kept no company," as the neighbours said. That was not so much the fault of the Athelings, as the simple fact that there was little company to keep; but they warmed the old heart of old Mr Foggo, and kept that singular personage on speaking terms with humanity; and day by day, and night by night, lived their frank life before their little world, a family life of love, activity, and cheerfulness, as bright to look at as their happy open parlour-window among the closed-up retirements of this genteel little street.

CHAPTER VII
THE FIRST WORK

"Now," said Agnes, throwing down her pen with a cry of triumph—"now, look here, everybody—it is done at last."

And, indeed, there it was upon the fair and legible page, in Agnes's best and clearest handwriting, "The End." She had written it with girlish delight, and importance worthy the occasion; and with admiring eyes Mamma and Marian looked upon the momentous words—The End! So now it was no longer in progress, to be smiled and wondered over, but an actual thing, accomplished and complete, out of anybody's power to check or to alter. The three came together to look at it with a little awe. It was actually finished—out of hand—an entire and single production. The last chapter was to be read in the family committee to-night—and then? They held their breath in sudden excitement. What was to be done with the Book, which could be smiled at no longer? That momentous question would have to be settled to-night.

So they piled it up solemnly, sheet by sheet, upon the side-table. Such a manuscript! Happy the printer into whose fortunate hands fell this unparalleled *copy*! And we are grieved to confess that, for the whole afternoon thereafter, Agnes Atheling was about as idle as it is possible even for a happy girl to be. No one but a girl could have attained to such a delightful eminence of doing nothing! She was somewhat unsettled, we admit, and quite uncontrollable,—dancing about everywhere, making her presence known by involuntary outbursts of singing and sweet laughter; but sterner lips than Mamma's would have hesitated to rebuke that fresh and spontaneous delight. It was not so much that she was glad to be done, or was relieved by the conclusion of her self-appointed labour. She did not, indeed, quite know what made her so happy. Like all primal gladness, it was involuntary and unexplainable; and the event of the day, vaguely exciting and exhilarating on its own account, was novel enough to supply that fresh breeze of excitement and change which is so pleasant always to the free heart of youth.

Then came all the usual routine of the evening—everything in its appointed time—from Susan, who brought the tea-tray, to Mr Foggo. And Mr Foggo stayed long, and was somewhat prosy. Agnes and Marian, for this one night, were sadly tired of the old gentleman, and bade him a very hasty and abrupt good-night when at last he took his departure. Even then, with a perverse inclination, Papa clung to his newspaper. The chances were much in favour of Agnes's dignified and stately withdrawal from an audience which showed so little eagerness for what she had to bestow upon them; but Marian, who was as much excited as Agnes, interposed. "Papa, Agnes is done—finished—done with her story—do you hear me, papa?" cried Marian in his ear, shaking him by the shoulder to give emphasis to her words—"she is going to read the last chapter, if you would lay down that stupid paper—do you hear, papa?"

Papa heard, but kept his finger at his place, and read steadily in spite of this interposition. "Be quiet, child," said the good Mr Atheling; but the child was not in the humour to be quiet. So after a few minutes, fairly persecuted out of his paper, Papa gave in, and threw it down; and the household circle closed round the fireside, and Agnes lifted her last chapter; but what that last chapter was, we are unable to tell, without infringing upon the privacy of Number Ten, Bellevue.

It was satisfactory—that was the great matter: everybody was satisfied with the annihilation of the impossible villain and the triumph of all the good people—and everybody concurred in thinking that the winding-up was as nearly perfect as it was in the nature of mortal winding-up to be. The MS. accordingly was laid aside, crowned with applauses and laurels;—then there was a pause of solemn consideration—the wise heads of the house held their peace and pondered. Marian, who was not wise, but only excited and impatient, broke the silence with her own eager, sincere, and unsolicited opinion; and this was the advice of Marian to the family committee of the whole house: "Mamma, I will tell you what ought to be done. It ought to be taken to somebody to-morrow, and published every month, like Dickens and Thackeray. It is quite as good! Everybody would read it, and Agnes would be a great author. I am quite sure that is the way."

At which speech Charlie whistled a very long "whew!" in a very low under-tone; for Mamma had very particular notions on the subject of "good-breeding," and kept careful watch over the "manners" even of this big boy.

"Like Dickens and Thackeray! Marian!" cried Agnes in horror; and then everybody laughed—partly because it was the grandest and most magnificent nonsense to place the young author upon this astonishing level, partly because it was so very funny to think of "our Agnes" sharing in ever so small a degree the fame of names like these.

"Not quite that," said Papa, slowly and doubtfully, "yet I think somebody might publish it. The question is, whom we should take it to. I think I ought to consult Foggo."

"Mr Foggo is not a literary man, papa," said Agnes, somewhat resentfully. She did not quite choose to receive this old gentleman, who thought her a child, into her confidence.

"Foggo knows a little of everything,—he has a wonderful head for business," said Mr Atheling. "As for a literary man, we do not know such a person, Agnes; and I can't see what better we should be if we did. Depend upon it, business is everything. If they think they can make money by this story of yours, they will take it, but not otherwise; for, of course, people trade in books as they trade in cotton, and are not a bit more generous in one than another, take my word for that."

"Very well, my dear," said Mamma, roused to assert her dignity, "but we do not wish any one to be generous to Agnes—of course not!—that would be out of the question; and nobody, you know, could look at that book without feeling sure of everybody else liking it. Why, William, it is so natural! You may speak of Thackeray and Dickens as you like; I know they are very clever—but I am sure I never read anything of theirs like that scene—that last scene with Helen and her mother. I feel as if I had been present there my own self."

Which was not so very wonderful after all, seeing that the mother in Agnes's book was but a delicate, shy, half-conscious sketch of this dearest mother of her own.

"I think it ought to be taken to somebody to-morrow," repeated Marian stoutly, "and published every month with pictures. How strange it would be to read in the newspapers how everybody wondered about the new book, and who wrote it!—such fun!—for nobody but *us* would know."

Agnes all this time remained very silent, receiving everybody's opinion—and Charlie also locked up his wisdom in his own breast. There was a pause, for Papa, feeling that his supreme opinion was urgently called for, took time to ponder upon it, and was rather afraid of giving a deliverance. The silence, however, was broken by the abrupt intervention, when nobody expected it, of the big boy.

"Make it up into a parcel," said Master Charlie with business-like distinctness, "and look in the papers what name you'll send it to, and I'll take it to-morrow."

This was so sudden, startling, and decisive, that the audience were electrified. Mr Atheling looked blankly in his son's face; the young gentleman had completely cut the ground from under the feet of his papa. After all, let any one advise or reason, or argue the point at his pleasure, this was the only practical conclusion to come at. Charlie stopped the full-tide of the family argument; they might have gone on till midnight discussing and wondering; but the big boy made it up into a parcel, and finished it on the spot. After that they all commenced a most ignorant and innocent discussion concerning "the trade;" these good people knew nothing whatever of that much contemned and long-suffering race who publish books. Two ideal types of them were present to the minds of the present speculators. One was that most fatal and fictitious savage, the Giant Despair of an oppressed literature, who sits in his den for ever grinding the bones of those dismal unforgettable hacks of Grub Street, whose memory clings unchangeably to their profession; the other was that bland and genial imagination, equally fictitious, the author's friend—he who brings the neglected genius into the full sunshine of fame and prosperity, seeking only the immortality of such a connection with the immortal. If one could only know which of these names in the newspapers belonged to this last wonder of nature! This discussion concerning people of whom absolutely nothing but the names were known to the disputants, was a very comical argument; and it was not concluded when eleven o'clock struck loudly on the kitchen clock, and Susan, very slumbrous, and somewhat resentful, appeared at the door to see if anything was wanted. Everybody rose immediately, as Susan intended they should, with guilt and confusion: eleven o'clock! the innocent family were ashamed of themselves.

And this little room up-stairs, as you do not need to be told, is the bower of Agnes and of Marian. There are two small white beds in it, white and fair and simple, draped with the purest dimity, and covered with the whitest coverlids. If Agnes, by chance or in haste—and Agnes is very often "in a great hurry"—should leave her share of the apartment in a less orderly condition than became a young lady's room, Marian never yielded to such a temptation. Marian was the completest woman in all her simple likings; their little mirror, their dressing-table, everything which would bear such fresh and inexpensive decoration, was draped with pretty muslin, the work of these pretty fingers. And there hung their little shelf of books over Agnes's head, and here upon the table was their Bible. Yet in spite of the quiet night settling towards midnight—in spite of the unbroken stillness of Bellevue, where every candle was extinguished, and all the world at rest, the girls could not subdue all at once their eager anticipations, hopes, and wondering. Marian let down all her beautiful hair over her shoulders, and pretended to brush it, looking all the time out of the shining veil, and throwing the half-curled locks from her face, when something occurred to her bearing upon the subject. Agnes, with both her hands supporting her forehead, leaned over the table with downcast eyes—seeing nothing, thinking nothing, with a faint glow on her soft cheek, and a vague excitement at her heart. Happy hearts! it was so easy to stir them to this sweet tumult of hope and fancy; and so small a reason was sufficient to wake these pure imaginations to all-indefinite glory and delight.

CHAPTER VIII
CHARLIE'S ENTERPRISE

It was made into a parcel, duly packed and tied up; not in a delicate wrapper, or with pretty ribbons, as perhaps the affectionate regard of Agnes might have suggested, but in the commonest and most matter-of-fact parcel imaginable. But by that time it began to be debated whether Charlie, after all, was a sufficiently dignified messenger. He was only a boy—that was not to be disputed; and Mrs Atheling did not think him at all remarkable for his "manners," and Papa doubted whether he was able to manage a matter of business. But, then, who could go?—not the girls certainly, and not their mother, who was somewhat timid out of her own house. Mr Atheling could not leave his office; and really, after all their objections, there was nobody but Charlie, unless it was Mr Foggo, whom Agnes would by no means consent to employ. So they brushed their big boy, as carefully as Moses Primrose was brushed before he went to the fair, and gave him strict injunctions to look as grave, as sensible, and as *old* as possible. All these commands Charlie received with perfect coolness, hoisting his parcel under his arm, and remaining entirely unmoved by the excitement around him. "I know well enough—don't be afraid," said Charlie; and he strode off like a young ogre, carrying Agnes's fortune under his arm. They all went to the window to look after him with some alarm and some hope; but though they were troubled for his youth, his abruptness, and his want of "manners," there was exhilaration in the steady ring of Charlie's manful foot, and his own entire and undoubting confidence. On he went, a boyish giant, to throw down that slender gage and challenge of the young genius to all the world. Meanwhile they returned to their private occupations, this little group of women, excited, doubtful, much expecting, marvelling over and over again what Mr Burlington would say. Such an eminence of lofty criticism and censorship these good people recognised in the position of Mr Burlington! He seemed to hold in his hands the universal key which opened everything: fame, honour, and reward, at that moment, appeared to these simple minds to be mere vassals of his pleasure; and all the balance of the future, as Agnes fancied, lay in the doubtful chance whether he was propitious or unpropitious. Simple imaginations! Mr Burlington, at that moment taking off his top-coat, and placing his easy-chair where no draught could reach it, was about as innocent of literature as Charlie Atheling himself.

But Charlie, who had to go to "the office" after he fulfilled his mission, could not come home till the evening; so they had to be patient in spite of themselves. The ordinary occupations of the day in Bellevue were not very novel, nor very interesting. Mrs Atheling had ambition, and aimed at gentility; so, of course, they had a piano. The girls had learned a very little music; and Marian and Agnes, when they were out of humour, or disinclined for serious occupation, or melancholy (for they were melancholy sometimes in the "prodigal excess" of their youth and happiness), were wont to bethink themselves of the much-neglected "practising," and spend a stray hour upon it with most inconsistent and variable zeal. This day there was a great deal of "practising"—indeed, these wayward girls divided their whole time between the piano and the garden, which was another recognised safety-valve. Mamma had not the heart to chide them; instead of that, her face brightened to hear the musical young voices, the low sweet laughter, the echo of their flying feet through the house and on the garden paths. As she sat at her work in her snug sitting-room, with Bell and Beau playing at her feet, and Agnes and Marian playing too, as truly, and with as pure and spontaneous delight, Mrs Atheling was very happy. She did not say a word that any one could hear—but God knew the atmosphere of unspoken and unspeakable gratitude, which was the very breath of this good woman's heart.

When their messenger came home, though he came earlier than Papa, and there was full opportunity to interrogate him—Charlie, we are grieved to say, was not very satisfactory in his communications. "Yes," said Charlie, "I saw him: I don't know if it was the head-man: of course, I asked for Mr Burlington—and he took the parcel—that's all."

"That's all?—you little savage!" cried Marian, who was not half as big as Charlie. "Did he say he would be glad to have it? Did he ask who had written it? What did he say?"

"Are you sure it was Mr Burlington?" said Agnes. "Did he look pleased? What do you think he thought? What did you say to him? Charlie, boy, tell us what you said?"

"I won't tell you a word, if you press upon me like that," said the big boy. "Sit down and be quiet. Mother, make them sit down. I don't know if it was Mr Burlington; I don't think it was: it was a washy man, that never could have been head of that place. He took the papers, and made a face at me, and said, 'Are they your own?' I said 'No' plain enough; and then he looked at the first page, and said they must be left. So I left them. Well, what was a man to do? Of course, that is all."

"What do you mean by making a face at you, boy?" said the watchful mother. "I do trust, Charlie, my dear, you were careful how to behave, and did not make any of your faces at him."

"Oh, it was only a smile," said Charlie, with again a grotesque imitation. "'Are they your own?'—meaning I was just a boy to be laughed at, you know—I should think so! As if I could not make an end of half-a-dozen like him."

"Don't brag, Charlie," said Marian, "and don't be angry about the gentleman, you silly boy; he always must have something on his mind different from a lad like you."

Charlie laughed with grim satisfaction. "He hasn't a great deal on his mind, that chap," said the big boy; "but I wouldn't be him, set up there for no end but reading rubbish—not for—five hundred a-year."

Now, we beg to explain that five hundred a-year was a perfectly magnificent income to the imagination of Bellevue. Charlie could not think at the moment of any greater inducement.

"Reading rubbish! And he has Agnes's book to read!" cried Marian. That was indeed an overpowering anti-climax.

"Yes, but how did he look? Do you think he was pleased? And will it be sure to come to Mr Burlington safe?" said Agnes. Agnes could not help having a secret impression that there might be some plot against this book of hers, and that everybody knew how important it was.

"Why, he looked—as other people look who have nothing to say," said Charlie; "and I had nothing to say—so we got on together. And he said it looked original—much he could tell from the first page! And so, of course, I came away—they're to write when they've read it over. I tell you, that's all. I don't believe it was Mr Burlington; but it was the man that does that sort of thing, and so it was all the same."

This was the substance of Charlie's report. He could not be prevailed upon to describe how this important critic looked, or if he was pleased, or anything about him. He was a washy man, Charlie said; but the obstinate boy would not even explain what washy meant, so they had to leave the question in the hands of time to bring elucidation to it. They were by no means patient; many and oft-repeated were the attacks upon Charlie— many the wonderings over the omnipotent personage who had the power of this decision in his keeping; but in the mean time, and for sundry days and weeks following, these hasty girls had to wait, and to be content.

CHAPTER IX
A DECISION

"I've been thinking," said Charlie Atheling slowly. Having made this preface, the big boy paused: it was his manner of opening an important subject, to which the greater part of his cogitations were directed. His sisters came close to him immediately, half-embracing this great fellow in their united arms, and waiting for his communication. It was the twilight of an April evening, soft and calm. There were no stars in the sky—no sky even, except an occasional break of clear deep heavenly blue through the shadowy misty shapes of clouds, crowding upon each other over the whole arch of heaven. The long boughs of the lilac-bushes rustled in the night wind with all their young soft leaves—the prim outline of the poplar was ruffled with brown buds, and low on the dark soil at its feet was a faint golden lustre of primroses. Everything was as still—not as death, for its deadly calm never exists in nature; but as life, breathing, hushing, sleeping in that sweet season, when the grass is growing and the bud unfolding, all the night and all the day. Even here, in this suburban garden, with the great Babel muffling its voices faintly in the far distance, you could hear, if you listened, that secret rustle of growth and renewing which belongs to the sweet spring. Even here, in this colourless soft light, you could see the earth opening her unwearied bosom, with a passive grateful sweetness, to the inspiring touch of heaven. The brown soil was moist with April showers, and the young leaves glistened faintly with blobs of dew. Very different from the noonday hope was this hope of twilight; but not less hopeful in its silent operations, its sweet sighs, its soft tears, and the heart that stirred within it, in the dark, like a startled bird.

These three young figures, closely grouped together, which you could see only in outline against the faint horizon and the misty sky, were as good a human rendering as could be made of the unexpressed sentiment of the season and the night—they too were growing, with a sweet involuntary progression, up to their life, and to their fate. They stood upon the threshold of the world innocent adventurers, fearing no evil; and it was hard to believe that these hopeful neophytes could ever be made into toil-worn, care-hardened people of the world by any sum of hardships or of years.

"I've been thinking;"—all this time Charlie Atheling had added nothing to his first remarkable statement, and we are compelled to admit that the conclusion which he now gave forth did not seem to justify the solemnity of the delivery—"yes, I've made up my mind; I'll go to old Foggo and the law."

"And why, Charlie, why?"

Charlie was not much given to rendering a reason.

"Never mind the why," he said, abruptly; "that's best. There's old Foggo himself, now; nobody can reckon his income, or make a balance just what he is and what he has, and all about him, as people could do with us. We are plain nobodies, and people know it at a glance. My father has five children and two hundred a-year—whereas old Foggo, you see—"

"*I* don't see—I do not believe it!" cried Marian, impatiently. "Do you mean to say, you bad boy, that Mr Foggo is better than papa—*my* father? Why, he has mamma, and Bell and Beau, and all of us: if anything ailed him, we should break our hearts. Mr Foggo has only Miss Willsie: he is an old man, and snuffs, and does not care for anybody: do you call *that* better than papa?"

But Charlie only laughed. Certain it was that this lad had not the remotest intention of setting up Mr Foggo as his model of happiness. Indeed, nobody quite knew what Charlie's ideal was; but the boy, spite of his practical nature, had a true boyish liking for that margin of uncertainty which made it possible to surmise some unknown power or greatness even in the person of this ancient lawyer's clerk. Few lads, we believe, among the range of those who have to make their own fortune, are satisfied at their outset to decide upon being "no better than papa."

"Well," said Agnes, with consideration, "I should not like Charlie to be just like papa. Papa can do nothing but keep us all—so many children—and he never can be anything more than he is now. But Charlie—Charlie is quite a different person. I wish he could be something great."

"Agnes—don't! it is such nonsense!" cried Marian. "Is there anything great in old Mr Foggo's office? He is a poor old man, *I* think, living all by himself with Miss Willsie. I had rather be Susan in our house, than be mistress in Mr Foggo's: and how could *he* make Charlie anything great?"

"Stuff!" said Charlie; "nobody wants to be *made*; that's a man's own business. Now, you just be quiet with your romancing, you girls. I'll tell you what, though, there's one man I think I'd like to be—and I suppose you call him great—I'd like to be Rajah Brooke."

"Oh, Charlie! and hang people!" cried Marian.

"Not people—only pirates," said the big boy: "wouldn't I string them up too! Yes, if that would please you, Agnes, I'd like to be Rajah Brooke."

"Then why, Charlie," exclaimed Agnes—"why do you go to Mr Foggo's office? A merchant may have a chance for such a thing—but a lawyer! Charlie, boy, what do you mean?"

"Never mind," said Charlie; "your Brookes and your Layards and such people don't begin by being merchants' clerks. I know better: they have birth and education, and all that, and get the start of everybody, and then they make a row about it. I don't see, for my part," said the young gentleman meditatively, "what it is but chance. A man may succeed, or a man may fail, and it's neither much to his credit nor his blame. It is a very odd thing, and I can't understand it—a man may work all his life, and never be the better for it. It's chance, and nothing more, so far as I can see."

"Hush, Charlie—say Providence," said Agnes, anxiously.

"Well, I don't know—it's very odd," answered the big boy.

Whereupon there began two brief but earnest lectures for the good of Charlie's mind, and the improvement of his sentiments. The girls were much disturbed by their brother's heterodoxy; they assaulted him vehemently with the enthusiastic eagerness of the young faith which had never been tried, and would not comprehend any questioning. Chance! when the very sparrows could not fall to the ground—The bright face of Agnes Atheling flushed almost into positive beauty; she asked indignantly, with a trembling voice and tears in her eyes, how Mamma could have endured to live if it had not been God who did it? Charlie, rough as he was, could not withstand an appeal like this: he muttered something hastily under his breath about success in business being a very different thing from *that*, and was indisputably overawed and vanquished. This allusion made them all very silent for a time, and the young bright eyes involuntarily glanced upward where the pure faint stars were gleaming out one by one among the vapoury hosts of cloud. Strangely touching was the solemnity of this link, not to be broken, which connected the family far down upon the homely bosom of the toilsome earth with yonder blessed children in the skies. Marian, saying nothing, wiped some tears silently from the beautiful eyes which turned such a wistful, wondering, longing look to the uncommunicating heaven. Charlie, though you could scarcely see him in the darkness, worked those heavy furrows of his brow, and frowned fiercely upon himself. The long branches came sweeping towards them, swayed by the night wind; up in the east rose the pale spring moon, pensive, with a misty halo like a saint. The aspect of the night was changed; instead of the soft brown gloaming, there was broad silvery light and heavy masses of shadow over sky and soil—an instant change all brought about by the rising of the moon. As swift an alteration had passed upon the mood of these young speculators. They went in silently, full of thought—not so sad but that they could brighten to the fireside brightness, yet more meditative than was their wont; even Charlie—for there was a warm heart within the clumsy form of this big boy!

CHAPTER X
MR FOGGO

They went in very sedately out of the darkness, their eyes dazzled with the sudden light. Bell and Beau were safely disposed of for the night, and on the side-table, beside Charlie's two grammars and Agnes's blotting-book, now nearly empty, lay the newspaper of Papa; for the usual visitor was installed in the usual place at the fireside, opposite Mr Atheling. Good companion, it is time you should see the friend of the family: there he was.

And there also, it must be confessed, was a certain faint yet expressive fragrance, which delicately intimated to one sense at least, before he made his appearance, the coming of Mr Foggo. We will not affirm that it was lundyfoot—our own private impression, indeed, is strongly in favour of black rappee—but the thing was indisputable, whatever might be the species. He was a large brown man, full of folds and wrinkles; folds in his brown waistcoat, where secret little sprinklings of snuff, scarcely perceptible, lay undisturbed and secure; wrinkles, long and forcible, about his mouth; folds under his eyelids, deep lines upon his brow. There was not a morsel of smooth surface visible anywhere even in his hands, which were traced all over with perceptible veins and sinews, like a geographical exercise. Mr Foggo wore a wig, which could not by any means be complimented with the same title as Mr Pendennis's "'cad of 'air." He was between fifty and sixty, a genuine old bachelor, perfectly satisfied with his own dry and unlovely existence. Yet we may suppose it was something in Mr Foggo's favour, the frequency of his visits here. He sat by the fireside with the home-air of one who knows that this chair is called his, and that he belongs to the household circle, and turned to look at the young people, as they entered, with a familiar yet critical eye. He was friendly enough, now and then, to deliver little rebukes and remonstrances, and was never complimentary, even to Marian; which may be explained, perhaps, when we say that he was a Scotsman—a north-country Scotsman—with "peculiarities" in his pronunciation, and very distinct opinions of his own. How he came to win his way into the very heart of this family, we are not able to explain; but there he was, and there Mr Foggo had been, summer and winter, for nearly half-a-score of years.

He was now an institution, recognised and respected. No one dreamt of investigating his claims—possession was the whole law in his case, his charter and legal standing-ground; and the young commonwealth recognised as undoubtingly the place of Mr Foggo as they did the natural throne and pre-eminence of Papa and Mamma.

"For my part," said Mr Foggo, who, it seemed, was in the midst of what Mrs Atheling called a "sensible conversation,"—and Mr Foggo spoke slowly, and with a certain methodical dignity,—"for my part, I see little in the art of politics, but just withholding as long as ye can, and giving as little as ye may; for a statesman, ye perceive, be he Radical or Tory, must ever consent to be a stout Conservative when he gets the upper hand. It's in the nature of things—it's like father and son—it's the primitive principle of government, if ye take my opinion. So I am never sanguine myself about a new ministry keeping its word. How should it keep its word? Making measures and opposing them are two as different things as can be. There's father and son, a standing example: the young man is the people and the old man is the government,—the lad spurs on and presses, the greybeard holds in and restrains."

"Ah, Foggo! all very well to talk," said Mr Atheling; "but men should keep their word, government or no government—that's what I say. Do you mean to tell me that a father would cheat his son with promises? No! no! no! Your excuses won't do for me."

"And as for speaking of the father and son, as if it was natural they should be opposed to each other, I am surprised at *you*, Mr Foggo," said Mrs Atheling, with emphatic disapproval. "There's my Charlie, now, a wilful boy; but do you think *he* would set his face against anything his papa or I might say?"

"Charlie," said Mr Foggo, with a twinkle of the grey-brown eye which shone clear and keen under folds of eyelid and thickets of eyebrow, "is an uncommon boy. I'm speaking of the general principle, not of exceptional cases. No! men and measures are well enough to make a noise or an election about; but to go against the first grand rule is not in the nature of man."

"Yes, yes!" said Mr Atheling, impatiently; "but I tell you he's broken his word—that's what I say—told a lie, neither more nor less. Do you mean to tell me that any general principle will excuse a man for breaking his promises? I challenge your philosophy for that."

"When ye accept promises that it's not in the nature of things a man can keep, ye must even be content with the alternative," said Mr Foggo.

"Oh! away with your nature of things!" cried Papa, who was unusually excited and vehement,—"scarcely civil," as Mrs Atheling assured him in her private reproof. "It's the nature of the man, that's what's wrong. False in youth, false in age,—if I had known!"

"Crooked ways are ill to get clear of," said Mr Foggo oracularly. "What's that you're about, Charlie, my boy? Take you my advice, lad, and never be a public man."

"A public man! I wish public men had just as much sense," said Mrs Atheling in an indignant under-tone. This good couple, like a great many other excellent people, were pleased to note how all the national businesses were mismanaged, and what miserable 'prentice-hands of pilots held the helm of State.

"I grant you it would not be overmuch for them," said Mr Foggo; "and speaking of government, Mrs Atheling, Willsie is in trouble again."

"I am very sorry," exclaimed Mrs Atheling, with instant interest. "Dear me, I thought this was such a likely person. You remember what I said to you, Agnes, whenever I saw her. She looked so neat and handy, I thought her quite the thing for Miss Willsie. What has she done?"

"Something like the Secretary of State for the Home Department," said Mr Foggo,—"made promises which could not be kept while she was on trial, and broke them when she took office. Shall I send the silly thing away?"

"Oh, Mr Foggo! Miss Willsie was so pleased with her last week—she could do so many things—she has so much good in her," cried Marian; "and then you can't tell—you have not tried her long enough—don't send her away!"

"She is so pretty, Mr Foggo," said Agnes.

Mr Foggo chuckled, thinking, not of Miss Willsie's maid-servant, but of the Secretary of State. Papa looked at him across the fireplace wrathfully. What the reason was, nobody could tell; but Papa was visibly angry, and in a most unamiable state of mind: he said "Tush!" with an impatient gesture, in answer to the chuckle of his opponent. Mr Atheling was really not at all polite to his friend and guest.

But we presume Mr Foggo was not sensitive—he only chuckled the more, and took a pinch of snuff. The snuff-box was a ponderous silver one, with an inscription on the lid, and always revealed itself most distinctly, in shape at least, within the brown waistcoat-pocket of its owner. As he enjoyed this refreshment, the odour diffused itself more distinctly through the apartment, and a powdery thin shower fell from Mr Foggo's huge brown fingers. Susan's cat, if she comes early to the parlour, will undoubtedly be seized with many sneezes to-morrow.

But Marian, who was innocently unconscious of any double meaning, continued to plead earnestly for Miss Willsie's maid. "Yes, Mr Foggo, she is so pretty," said Marian, "and so neat, and smiles. I am sure Miss Willsie herself would be grieved after, if she sent her away. Let mamma speak to Miss Willsie, Mr Foggo. She smiles as if she could not help it. I am sure she is good. Do not let Miss Willsie send her away."

"Willsie is like the public—she is never content with her servants," said Mr Foggo. "Where's all the poetry to-night? no ink upon Agnes's finger! I don't understand that."

"I never write poetry, Mr Foggo," said Agnes, with superb disdain. Agnes was extremely annoyed by Mr Foggo's half-knowledge of her authorship. The old gentleman took her for one of the young ladies who write verses, she thought; and for this most amiable and numerous sisterhood, the young genius, in her present mood, had a considerable disdain.

"And ink on her finger! You never saw ink on Agnes's finger—you know you never did!" cried the indignant Marian. "If she did write poetry, it is no harm; and I know very well you only mean to tease her: but it is wrong to say what never was true."

Mr Foggo rose, diffusing on every side another puff of his peculiar element. "When I have quarrelled with everybody, I reckon it is about time to go home," said Mr Foggo. "Charlie, step across with me, and get some nonsense-verses Willsie has been reading, for the girls. Keep in the same mind, Agnes, and never write poetry—it's a mystery; no man should meddle with it till he's forty—that's *my* opinion—and then there would be as few poets as there are Secretaries of State."

"Secretaries of State!" exclaimed Papa, restraining his vehemence, however, till Mr Foggo was fairly gone, and out of hearing—and then Mr Atheling made a pause. You could not suppose that his next observation had any reference to this indignant exclamation; it was so oddly out of connection that even the girls smiled to each other. "I tell you what, Mary, a man should not be led by fantastic notions—a man should never do anything that does not come directly in his way," said Mr Atheling, and he pushed his grizzled hair back from his brow with heat and excitement. It was an ordinary saying enough, not much to be marvelled at. What did Papa mean?

"Then, papa, nothing generous would ever be done in the world," said Marian, who, somewhat excited by Mr Foggo, was quite ready for an argument on any subject, or with any person.

"But things that have to be done always come in people's way," said Agnes; "is not that true? I am sure, when you read people's lives, the thing they have to do seems to pursue them; and even if they do not want it, they cannot help themselves. Papa, is not that true?"

"Ay, ay—hush, children," said Mr Atheling, vaguely; "I am busy—speak to your mother."

They spoke to their mother, but not of this subject. They spoke of Miss Willsie's new maid, and conspired together to hinder her going away; and then they marvelled somewhat over the book which Charlie was to bring home. Mr Foggo and his maiden sister lived in Bellevue, in one of the villas semi-detached, which Miss Willsie had named Killiecrankie Lodge, yet Charlie was some time absent. "He is talking to Mr Foggo, instead of bringing our book," said Marian, pouting with her pretty lips. Papa and Mamma had each of them settled into a brown study—a very brown study, to judge from appearances. The fire was low—the lights looked dim. Neither of the girls were doing anything, save waiting on Charlie. They were half disposed to be peevish. "It is not too late; come and practise for half an hour, Agnes," said Marian, suddenly. Mrs Atheling was too much occupied to suggest, as she usually did, that the music would wake Bell and Beau: they stole away from the family apartment unchidden and undetained, and, lighting another candle, entered the genteel and solemn darkness of the best room. You have not been in the best room; let us enter with due dignity this reserved and sacred apartment, which very few people ever enter, and listen to the music which nobody ever hears.

CHAPTER XI
THE BEST ROOM

The music, we are grieved to say, was not at all worth listening to—it would not have disturbed Bell and Beau had the two little beds been on the top of the piano. Though Marian with a careless hand ran over three or four notes, the momentary sound did not disturb the brown study of Mrs Atheling, and scarcely roused Susan, nodding and dozing, as she mended stockings by the kitchen fire. We are afraid this same practising was often an excuse for half an hour's idleness and dreaming. Sweet idleness! happy visions! for it certainly was so to-night.

The best room was of the same size exactly as the family sitting-room, but looked larger by means of looking prim, chill, and uninhabited—and it was by no means crowded with furniture. The piano in one corner and a large old-fashioned table in another, with a big leaf of black and bright mahogany folded down, were the only considerable articles in the room, and the wall looked very blank with its array of chairs. The sofa inclined towards the unlighted fire, and the round table stood before it; but you could not delude yourself into the idea that this at any time could be the family hearth. Mrs Atheling "kept no company;" so, like other good people in the same condition, she religiously preserved and kept in order the company-room; and it was a comfort to her heart to recollect that in this roomy house there was always an orderly place where strangers could be shown into, although the said strangers never came.

The one candle had been placed drearily among the little coloured glass vases on the mantel-shelf; but the moonlight shone broad and full into the window, and, pouring its rays over the whole visible scene without, made something grand and solemn even of this genteel and silent Bellevue. The tranquil whiteness on these humble roofs—the distinctness with which one branch here and there, detached and taken possession of by the light, marked out its half-developed buds against the sky—the strange magic which made that faint ascending streak of smoke the ethereal plaything of these moonbeams—and the intense blackness of the shadow, deep as though it fell from one of the pyramids, of these homely garden-walls—made a wonderful and striking picture of a scene which had not one remarkable feature of its own; and the solitary figure crossing the road, all enshrined and hallowed in this silvery glory, but itself so dark and undistinguishable, was like a figure in a vision—an emblematic and symbolical appearance, entering like a picture to the spectator's memory. The two girls stood looking out, with their arms entwined, and their fair heads close together, as is the wont of such companions, watching the wayfarer, whose weary footstep was inaudible in the great hush and whisper of the night.

"I always fancy one might see ghosts in moonlight," said Marian, under her breath. Certainly that solitary passenger, with all the silvered folds of his dress, and the gliding and noiseless motion of his progress, was not entirely unlike one.

"He looks like a man in a parable," said Agnes, in the same tone. "One could think he was gliding away mysteriously to do something wrong. See, now, he has gone into the shadow. I cannot see him at all—he has quite disappeared—it is so black. Ah! I shall think he is always standing there, looking over at us, and plotting something. I wish Charlie would come home—how long he is!"

"Who would plot anything against us?" said innocent Marian, with her fearless smile. "People do not have enemies now as they used to have—at least not common people. I wish he would come out again, though, out of that darkness. I wonder what sort of man he could be."

But Agnes was no longer following the man; her eye was wandering vaguely over the pale illumination of the sky. "I wonder what will happen to us all?" said Agnes, with a sigh—sweet sigh of girlish thought that knew no care! "I think we are all beginning now, Marian, every one of us. I wonder what will happen—Charlie and all?"

"Oh, I can tell you," said Marian; "and you first of all, because you are the eldest. We shall all be famous, Agnes, every one of us; all because of you."

"Oh, hush!" cried Agnes, a smile and a flush and a sudden brightness running over all her face; "but suppose it *should* be so, you know, Marian— only suppose it for our own pleasure—what a delight it would be! It might help Charlie on better than anything; and then what we could do for Bell and Beau! Of course it is nonsense," said Agnes, with a low laugh and a sigh of excitement, "but how pleasant it would be!"

"It is not nonsense at all; I think it is quite certain," said Marian; "but then people would seek you out, and you would have to go and visit them— great people—clever people. Would it not be odd to hear real ladies and gentlemen talking in company as they talk in books?"

"I wonder if they do," said Agnes, doubtfully. "And then to meet people whom we have heard of all our lives—perhaps Bulwer even!—perhaps Tennyson! Oh, Marian!"

"And to know they were very glad to meet *you*," exclaimed the sister dreamer, with another low laugh of absolute pleasure: that was very near the climax of all imaginable honours—and for very awe and delight the young visionaries held their breath.

"And I think now," said Marian, after a little interval, "that perhaps it is better Charlie should be a lawyer, for he would have so little at first in papa's office, and he never could get on, more than papa; and you would not like to leave all the rest of us behind you, Agnes? I know you would not. But I hope Charlie will never grow like Mr Foggo, so old and solitary; to be poor would be better than that."

"Then I could be Miss Willsie," said Agnes, "and we should live in a little square house, with two bits of lawn and two fir-trees; but I think we would not call it Killiecrankie Lodge."

Over this felicitous prospect there was a great deal of very quiet laughing—laughing as sweet and as irrepressible as any other natural music, but certainly not evidencing any very serious purpose on the part of either of the young sisters to follow the example of Miss Willsie. They had so little thought, in their fair unconscious youth, of all the long array of years and changes which lay between their sweet estate and that of the restless kind old lady, the mistress of Mr Foggo's little square house.

"And then, for me—what should I do?" said Marian. There were smiles hiding in every line of this young beautiful face, curving the pretty eyebrow, moving the soft lip, shining shy and bright in the sweet eyes. No anxiety—not the shadow of a shade—had ever crossed this young girl's imagination touching her future lot. It was as rosy as the west and the south, and the cheeks of Maud in Mr Tennyson's poem. She had no thought of investigating it too closely; it was all as bright as a summer day to Marian, and she was ready to spend all her smiles upon the prediction, whether it was ill or well.

"Then I suppose you must be married, May. I see nothing else for you," said Agnes, "for there could not possibly be two Miss Willsies; but I should like to see, in a fairy glass, who my other brother was to be. He must be clever, Marian, and it would be very pleasant if he could be rich, and I suppose he ought to be handsome too."

"Oh, Agnes! handsome of course, first of all!" cried Marian, laughing, "nobody but you would put that last."

"But then I rather like ugly people, especially if they are clever," said Agnes; "there is Charlie, for example. If he was *very* ugly, what an odd couple you would be!—he ought to be ugly for a balance—and very witty and very pleasant, and ready to do anything for you, May. Then if he were only rich, and you could have a carriage, and be a great lady, I think I should be quite content."

"Hush, Agnes! mamma will hear you—and now there is Charlie with a book," said Marian. "Look! he is quite as mysterious in the moonlight as the other man—only Charlie could never be like a ghost—and I wonder what the book is. Come, Agnes, open the door."

This was the conclusion of the half-hour's practising; they made grievously little progress with their music, yet it was by no means an unpleasant half-hour.

CHAPTER XII
A SERIOUS QUESTION

Mrs Atheling has been calling upon Miss Willsie, partly to intercede for Hannah, the pretty maid, partly on a neighbourly errand of ordinary gossip and kindliness; but in decided excitement and agitation of mind Mamma has come home. It is easy to perceive this as she hurries up-stairs to take off her shawl and bonnet; very easy to notice the fact, as, absent and preoccupied, she comes down again. Bell and Beau are in the kitchen, and the kitchen-door is open. Bell has Susan's cat, who is very like to scratch her, hugged close in her chubby arms. Beau hovers so near the fire, on which there is no guard, that his mother would think him doomed did she see him; but—it is true, although it is almost unbelievable—Mamma actually passes the open kitchen-door without observing either Bell or Beau!

The apples of her eye! Mrs Atheling has surely something very important to occupy her thoughts; and now she takes her usual chair, but does not attempt to find her work-basket. What can possibly have happened to Mamma?

The girls have not to wait very long in uncertainty. The good mother speaks, though she does not distinctly address either of them. "They want a lad like Charlie in Mr Foggo's office," said Mrs Atheling. "I knew that, and that Charlie could have the place; but they also want an articled clerk."

"An articled clerk!—what is that, mamma?" said Agnes, eagerly.

To tell the truth, Mrs Atheling did not very well know what it was, but she knew it was "something superior," and that was enough for her motherly ambition.

"Well, my dear, it is a gentleman," said Mrs Atheling, "and of course there must be far greater opportunities of learning. It is a superior thing altogether, I believe. Now, being such old friends, I should think Mr Foggo might get them to take a very small premium. Such a thing for Charlie! I am sure we could all pinch for a year or two to give him a beginning like *that!*"

"Would it be much better, mamma?" said Marian. They had left what they were doing to come closer about her, pursuing their eager interrogations.

Marian sat down upon a stool on the rug where the fire-light brightened her hair and reddened her cheek at its pleasure. Agnes stood on the opposite side of the hearth, looking down upon the other interlocutors. They were impatient to hear all that Mrs Atheling had heard, and perfectly ready to jump to an unanimous opinion.

"Better, my dear!" said Mrs Atheling—"just as much better as a young man learning to be a master can be better than one who is only a servant. Then, you know, it would give Charlie standing, and get him friends of a higher class. I think it would be positively a sin to neglect such an opportunity; we might never all our lives hear of anything like it again."

"And how did you hear of it, mamma?" said Marian. Marian had quite a genius for asking questions.

"I heard of it from Miss Willsie, my love. It was entirely by accident. She was telling me of an articled pupil they had at the office, who had gone all wrong, poor fellow, in consequence of— —; but I can tell you that another time. And then she said they wanted one now, and then it flashed upon me just like an inspiration. I was quite agitated. I do really declare to you, girls, I thought it was Providence; and I believe, if we only were bold enough to do it in faith, God would provide the means; and I feel sure it would be the making of Charlie. I think so indeed."

"I wonder what he would say himself?" said Agnes; for not even Mrs Atheling knew so well as Agnes did the immovable determination, when he had settled upon anything, of this obstinate big boy.

"We will speak of it to-night, and see what your papa says, and I would not mind even mentioning it to Mr Foggo," said Mrs Atheling: "we have not very much to spare, yet I think we could all spare something for Charlie's sake; we must have it fully discussed to-night."

This made, for the time, a conclusion of the subject, since Mrs Atheling, having unburthened her mind to her daughters, immediately discovered the absence of the children, rebuked the girls for suffering them to stray, and set out to bring them back without delay. Marian sat musing before the fire, scorching her pretty cheek with the greatest equanimity. Agnes threw herself into Papa's easy-chair. Both hurried off immediately into delightful speculations touching Charlie—a lawyer and a gentleman; and already in their secret hearts both of these rash girls began to entertain the utmost contempt for the commonplace name of clerk.

We are afraid Mr Atheling's tea was made very hurriedly that night. He could not get peace to finish his third cup, that excellent papa: they persecuted him out of his ordinary play with Bell and Beau; his invariable study of the newspaper. He could by no means make out the cause of the commotion. "Not another story finished already, Agnes?" said the perplexed head of the house. He began to think it would be something rather alarming if they succeeded each other like this.

"Now, my dears, sit down, and do not make a noise with your work, I beg of you. I have something to say to your papa," said Mrs Atheling, with state and solemnity.

Whereupon Papa involuntarily put himself on his defence; he had not the slightest idea what could be amiss, but he recognised the gravity of the preamble. "What *is* the matter, Mary?" cried poor Mr Atheling. He could not tell what he had done to deserve this.

"My dear, I want to speak about Charlie," said Mrs Atheling, becoming now less dignified, and showing a little agitation. "I went to call on Miss Willsie to-day, partly about Hannah, partly for other things; and Miss Willsie told me, William, that besides the youth's place which we thought would do for Charlie, there was in Mr Foggo's office a vacancy for an articled clerk."

Mrs Atheling paused, out of breath. She did not often make long speeches, nor had she frequently before originated and led a great movement like this, so she showed fully as much excitement as the occasion required. Papa listened with composure and a little surprise, relieved to find that he was not on his trial. Charlie pricked his big red ears, as he sat at his grammar, but made no other sign; while the girls, altogether suspending their work, drew their chairs closer, and with a kindred excitement eagerly followed every word and gesture of Mamma.

"And you must see, William," said Mrs Atheling, rapidly, "what a great advantage it would be to Charlie, if he could enter the office like a gentleman. Of course, I know he would get no salary; but we could go on very well for a year or two as we are doing—quite as well as before, certainly; and I have no doubt Mr Foggo could persuade them to be content with a very small premium; and then think of the advantage to Charlie, my dear!"

"Premium! no salary!—get on for a year or two! Are you dreaming, Mary?" exclaimed Mr Atheling. "Why, this is a perfect craze, my dear. Charlie an articled clerk in Foggo's office! it is pure nonsense. You don't mean to say such a thought has ever taken possession of *you*. I could understand the girls, if it was their notion—but, Mary! you!"

"And why not me?" said Mamma, somewhat angry for the moment. "Who is so anxious as me for my boy? I know what our income is, and what it can do exactly to a penny, William—a great deal better than you do, my dear; and of course it would be my business to draw in our expenses accordingly; and the girls would give up anything for Charlie's sake. And then, except Beau, who is so little, and will not want anything much done for him for many a year—he is our only boy, William. It was not always so," said the good mother, checking a great sob which had nearly stopped her voice—"it was not always so—but there is only Charlie left of all of them; and except little Beau, the son of our old age, he is our only boy!"

She paused now, because she could not help it; and for the same reason her husband was very slow to answer. All-prevailing was this woman's argument; it was very near impossible to say the gentlest Nay to anything thus pleaded in the name of the dead.

"But, my dear, we cannot do it," said Mr Atheling very quietly. The good man would have given his right hand at that moment to be able to procure this pleasure for the faithful mother of those fair boys who were in heaven.

"We could do it if we tried, William," said Mrs Atheling, recovering herself slowly. Her husband shook his head, pondered, shook his head again.

"It would be injustice to the other children," he said at last. "We could not keep Charlie like a gentleman without injuring the rest. I am surprised you do not think of that."

"But the rest of us are glad to be injured," cried Agnes, coming to her mother's aid; "and then I may have something by-and-by, and Charlie could get on so much better. I am sure you must see all the advantages, papa."

"And we can't be injured either, for we shall just be as we are," said Marian, "only a little more economical; and I am sure, papa, if it is so great a virtue to be thrifty, as you and Mr Foggo say, you ought to be more anxious than we are about this for Charlie; and you would, if you carried out your principles—and you must submit. I know we shall succeed at last."

"If it is a conspiracy, I give in," said Mr Atheling. "Of course you must mulct yourselves if you have made up your minds to it. I protest against suffering your thrift myself, and I won't have any more economy in respect to Bell and Beau. But do your will, Mary—I don't interfere. A conspiracy is too much for me."

"Mother!" said Charlie—all this time there had been nothing visible of the big boy, except the aforesaid red ears; now he put down his grammar and came forward, with some invisible wind working much among the furrows of his brow—"just hear what I've got to say. This won't do—I'm not a gentleman, you know; what's the good of making me like one?—of course I mean," said Charlie, somewhat hotly, in a parenthesis, as Agnes's eyes flashed upon him, "not a gentleman, so far as being idle and having plenty of money goes;—I've got to work for my bread. Suppose I was articled, at the end of my time I should have to work for my bread all the same. What is the difference? It's only making a sham for two years, or three years, or whatever the time might be. I don't want to go against what anybody says, but you wouldn't make a sham of me, would you, mother? Let me go in my proper place—like what I'll have to be, all my life; then if I rise you will be pleased; and if I don't rise, still nobody will be able to say I have come down. I can't be like a gentleman's son, doing nothing. Let me be myself, mother—the best thing for me."

Charlie said scarcely any more that night, though much was said on every side around; but Charlie was the conqueror.

CHAPTER XIII
KILLIECRANKIE LODGE

Killiecrankie Lodge held a dignified position in this genteel locality: it stood at the end of the road, looking down and superintending Bellevue. Three square houses, all duly walled and gardened, made the apex and conclusion of this suburban retirement. The right-hand one was called Buena Vista House; the left-hand one was Green View Cottage, and in the centre stood the lodge of Killiecrankie. The lodge was not so jealously private as its neighbours: in the upper part of the door in the wall was an open iron railing, through which the curious passenger might gain a beatific glimpse of Miss Willsie's wallflowers, and of the clean white steps by which you ascended to the house-door. The corresponding loopholes at the outer entrance of Green View and Buena Vista were carefully boarded; so the house of Mr Foggo had the sole distinction of an open eye.

Within the wall was a paved path leading to the house, with a square bit of lawn on either side, each containing in its centre a very small round flower-plot and a minute fir-tree. These were the pine forests of the Islingtonian Killiecrankie; but there were better things within the brief enclosure. The borders round about on every side were full of wallflowers—double wallflower, streaked wallflower, yellow wallflower, brown wallflower—every variety under the sun. This was the sole remarkable instance of taste displayed by Miss Willsie; but it gave a delicate tone of fragrance to the whole atmosphere of Bellevue.

This is a great day at Killiecrankie Lodge. It is the end of April now, and already the days are long, and the sun himself stays up till after tea, and throws a slanting golden beam over the daylight table. Miss Willsie, herself presiding, is slightly heated. She says, "Bless me, it's like July!" as she sets down upon the tray her heavy silver teapot. Miss Willsie is not half as tall as her brother, but makes up the difference in another direction. She is stout, though she is so restlessly active. Her face is full of wavering little lines and dimples, though she is an old lady; and there are the funniest indentations possible in her round chin and cheeks. You would fancy a laugh was always hiding in those crevices. Alas! Hannah knows better. You should see how Miss Willsie can frown!

But the old lady is in grand costume to-night; she has her brown satin dress on, her immense cairngorm brooch, her overwhelming blue turban. This sublime head-dress has an effect of awe upon the company; no one was prepared for such a degree of grandeur, and the visitors consequently are not quite at their ease. These visitors are rather numerous for a Bellevue tea-party. There is Mr Richards from Buena Vista, Mrs Tavistock from Woburn Lodge, and Mr Gray, the other Scotch inhabitant, from Gowanbrae; and there is likewise Mr Foggo Silas Endicott, Miss Willsie's American nephew, and her Scotch nephew, Harry Oswald; and besides all this worshipful company, there are all the Athelings—all except Bell and Beau, left, with many cautions, in the hands of Susan, over whom, in fear and self-reproach, trembles already the heart of Mamma.

"So he would not hear of it—he was not blate!" said Miss Willsie. "My brother never had the like in his office—that I tell you; and there's no good mother at home to do as much for Harry. Chairles, lad, you'll find out better some time. If there's one thing I do not like, it's a wilful boy!"

"But I can scarcely call him wilful either," said Mrs Atheling, hastily. "He is very reasonable, Miss Willsie; he gives his meaning—it is not out of opposition. He has always a good reason for what he does—he is a very reasonable boy."

"And if there's one thing I object to," said Miss Willsie, "it's the assurance of these monkeys with their reasons. When we were young, we were ill bairns, doubtless, like other folk; but if I had dared to make my excuses, pity me! There is Harry, now, will set up his face to me as grand as a Lord of Session; and Marian this very last night making her argument about these two spoiled babies of yours, as if she knew better than me! Misbehaviour's natural to youth. I can put up with that, but I cannot away with their reasons. Such things are not for me."

"Very true—*so* true, Miss Willsie," said Mrs Tavistock, who was a sentimental and sighing widow. "There is my niece, quite an example. I am sadly nervous, you know; and that rude girl will 'prove' to me, as she calls it, that no thief could get into the house, though I know they try the back-kitchen window every night."

"If there's one thing I'm against," said Miss Willsie, solemnly, "it's that foolish fright about thieves—thieves! Bless me, what would the ragamuffins do here? A man may be a robber, but that's no to say he's an idiot; and a wise man would never put his life or his freedom in jeopardy for what he could get in Bellevue."

Mrs Tavistock was no match for Miss Willsie, so she prudently abstained from a rejoinder. A large old china basin full of wallflowers stood under a grim portrait, and between a couple of huge old silver candlesticks upon the mantelpiece; Miss Willsie's ancient tea-service, at present glittering upon the table, was valuable and massive silver: nowhere else in Bellevue was there so much "plate" as in Killiecrankie Lodge; and this was perfectly well known to the nervous widow. "I am sure I wonder at your courage, Miss Willsie; but then you have a gentleman in the house, which makes a great difference," said Mrs Tavistock, woefully. Mrs Tavistock was one of those proper and conscientious ladies who make a profession of their widowhood, and are perpetually executing a moral suttee to the edification of all beholders. "I was never nervous before. Ah, nobody knows what a difference it makes to me!"

"Young folk are a troublesome handful. Where are the girls—what are they doing with Harry?" said Miss Willsie. "Harry's a lad for any kind of antics, but you'll no see Foggo demeaning himself. Foggo writes poems and letters to the papers: they tell me that in his own country he's a very rising young man."

"He looks intellectual. What a pleasure, Miss Willsie, to you!" said the widow, with delightful sympathy.

"If there's one thing I like worse than another, it's your writing young men," said Miss Willsie, vehemently. "I lighted on a paper this very day, that the young leasing-maker had gotten from America, and what do you think I saw therein, but just a long account—everything about us—of my brother and me. My brother Robert Foggo, as decent a man as there is in the three kingdoms—and *me*! What do you think of that, Mrs Atheling?—even Harry in it, and the wallflowers! If it had not been for my brother, he never should have set foot in this house again."

"Oh dear, how interesting!" said the widow. Mrs Tavistock turned her eyes to the other end of the room almost with excitement. She had not the least objection, for her own part, in the full pomp of sables and sentiment, to figure at full length in the *Mississippi Gazette*.

"And what was it for?" said Mrs Atheling, innocently; "for I thought it was only remarkable people that even the Americans put in the papers. Was it simply to annoy you?"

"Me!—do you think a lad like yon could trouble *me*?" exclaimed Miss Willsie. "He says, 'All the scenes through which he has passed will be interesting to his readers.' That's in a grand note he sent me this morning— the impertinent boy! My poor Harry, though he's often in mischief, and my brother thinks him unsteady—I would not give his little finger for half-a-dozen lads like yon."

"But Harry is doing well *now*, Miss Willsie?" said Mrs Atheling. There was a faint emphasis on the now which proved that Harry had not always done well.

"Ay," said Miss Willsie, drily; "and so Chairles has settled to his business—that's aye a comfort. If there's one thing that troubles me, it is to see young folk growing up in idleness; I pity them, now, that are genteel and have daughters. What are you going to do, Mrs Atheling, with these girls of yours?"

Mrs Atheling's eyes sought them out with fond yet not untroubled observation. There was Marian's beautiful head before the other window, looking as if it had arrested and detained the sunbeams, long ago departed in the west; and there was Agnes, graceful, animated, and intelligent, watching, with an affectionate and only half-conscious admiration, her sister's beauty. Their mother smiled to herself and sighed. Even her anxiety, looking at them thus, was but another name for delight.

"Agnes," said Marian at the other window, half whispering, half aloud—"Agnes! Harry says Mr Endicott has published a book."

With a slight start and a slight blush Agnes turned round. Mr Foggo S. Endicott was tall, very thin, had an extremely lofty mien, and a pair of spectacles. He was eight-and-twenty, whiskerless, sallow, and by no means handsome: he held his thin head very high, and delivered his sentiments into the air when he spoke, but rarely bent from his altitude to address any one in particular. But he heard the whisper in a moment: in his very elbows, as you stood behind him, you could see the sudden consciousness. He perceived, though he did not look at her, the eager, bright, blushing, half-reverential glance of Agnes, and, conscious to his very finger-points, raised his thin head to its fullest elevation, and pretended not to hear.

Agnes blushed: it was with sudden interest, curiosity, reverence, made more personal and exciting by her own venture. Nothing had been heard yet of this venture, though it was nearly a month since Charlie took it to Mr Burlington, and the young genius looked with humble and earnest attention upon one who really had been permitted to make his utterance to the ear of all the world. He *had* published a book; he was a real genuine printed author. The lips of Agnes parted with a quick breath of eagerness; she looked up at him with a blush on her cheek, and a light in her eye. A thrill of wonder and excitement came over her: would people by-and-by regard herself in the same light?

"Oh, Mr Endicott!—is it poems?" said Agnes, shyly, and with a deepening colour. The simple girl was almost as much embarrassed asking him about his book, as if she had been asking about the Transatlantic lady of this Yankee young gentleman's love.

"Oh!" said Mr Endicott, discovering suddenly that she addressed him— "yes. Did you speak to me?—poems?—ah! some little fugitive matters, to be sure. One has no right to refuse to publish, when everybody comes to know that one does such things."

"Refuse?—no, indeed; I think not," said Agnes, in spite of herself feeling very much humbled, and speaking very low. This was so elevated a view of the matter, and her own was so commonplace a one, that the poor girl was completely crestfallen. She so anxious to get into print; and this *bonâ fide* author, doubtless so very much her superior, explaining how he submitted, and could not help himself! Agnes was entirely put down.

"Yes, really one ought not to keep everything for one's own private enjoyment," said the magnanimous Mr Endicott, speaking very high up into the air with his cadenced voice. "I do not approve of too much reserve on the part of an author myself."

"And what are they about, Mr Endicott?" asked Marian, with respect, but by no means so reverentially as Agnes. Mr Endicott actually looked at Marian; perhaps it was because of her very prosaic and improper question, perhaps for the sake of the beautiful face.

"About!" said the poet, with benignant disdain. "No, I don't approve of narrative poetry; it's after the time. My sonnets are experiences. I live them before I write them; that is the true secret of poetry in our enlightened days."

Agnes listened, much impressed and cast down. She was far too simple to perceive how much superior her natural bright impulse, spontaneous and effusive, was to this sublime concentration. Agnes all her life long had never lived a sonnet; but she was so sincere and single-minded herself, that, at the first moment of hearing it, she received all this nonsense with unhesitating faith. For she had not yet learned to believe in the possibility of anybody, save villains in books, saying anything which they did not thoroughly hold as true.

So Agnes retired a little from the conversation. The young genius began to take herself to task, and was much humiliated by the contrast. Why had she written that famous story, now lying storm-stayed in the hands of Mr Burlington? Partly to please herself—partly to please Mamma—partly because she could not help it. There was no grand motive in the whole matter. Agnes looked with reverence at Mr Endicott, and sat down in a corner. She would have been completely conquered if the sublime American had been content to hold his peace.

But this was the last thing which occurred to Mr Endicott. He continued his utterances, and the discouraged girl began to smile. She was no judge of character, but she began to be able to distinguish nonsense when she heard it. This was very grand nonsense on the first time of hearing, and Agnes and Marian, we are obliged to confess, were somewhat annoyed when Mamma made a movement of departure. They kept very early hours in Bellevue, and before ten o'clock all Miss Willsie's guests had said good-night to Killiecrankie Lodge.

CHAPTER XIV
THE HOUSE OF FOGGO

It was ten o'clock, and now only this little family circle was left in the Lodge of Killiecrankie. Miss Willsie, with one of the big silver candlesticks drawn so very close that her blue turban trembled, and stood in jeopardy, read the *Times*; Mr Foggo sat in his armchair, doing nothing save contemplating the other light in the other candlestick; and at the unoccupied sides of the table, between the seniors, were the two young men.

These nephews did not live at Killiecrankie Lodge; but Miss Willsie, who was very careful, and a notable manager, considered it would be unsafe for "the boys" to go home to their lodgings at so late an hour as this—so her invitations always included a night's lodging; and the kind and arbitrary little woman was not accustomed to be disobeyed. Yet "the boys" found it dull, we confess. Mr Foggo was not pleased with Harry, and by no means "took" to Endicott. Miss Willsie could not deny herself her evening's reading. They yawned at each other, these unfortunate young men, and with a glance of mutual jealousy thought of Marian Atheling. It was strange to see how dull and disenchanted this place looked when the beautiful face that brightened it was gone.

So Mr Foggo S. Endicott took from his pocket his own paper, the *Mississippi Gazette*, and Harry possessed himself of the half of Miss Willsie's *Times*. It was odd to observe the difference between them even in manner and attitude. Harry bent half over the table, with his hands thrust up into the thick masses of his curling hair; the American sat perfectly upright, lifting his thin broadsheet to the height of his spectacles, and reading loftily his own lucubrations. You could scarcely see the handsome face of Harry as he hung over his half of the paper, partly reading, partly dreaming over certain fond fancies of his own; but you could not only see the lofty lineaments of Foggo, which were not at all handsome, but also could perceive at a glance that he had "a remarkable profile," and silently called your attention to it. Unfortunately, nobody in the present company was at all concerned about the profile of Mr Endicott. That philosophical young gentleman, notwithstanding, read his "Letter from England" in his best manner, and demeaned himself as loftily as if he were a "portrait of a distinguished literary gentleman" in an American museum. What more could any man do?

Meanwhile Mr Foggo sat in his armchair steadily regarding the candle before him. He loved conversation, but he was not talkative, especially in his own house. Sometimes the old man's acute eyes glanced from under his shaggy brow with a momentary keenness towards Harry—sometimes they shot across the table a momentary sparkle of grim contempt; but to make out from Mr Foggo's face what Mr Foggo was thinking, was about the vainest enterprise in the world. It was different with his sister: Miss Willsie's well-complexioned countenance changed and varied like the sky. You could pursue her sudden flashes of satisfaction, resentment, compassion, and injury into all her dimples, as easily as you could follow the clouds over the heavens. Nor was it by her looks alone that you could discover the fluctuating sympathies of Miss Willsie. Short, abrupt, hasty exclamations, broke from her perpetually. "The vagabond!—to think of that!" "Ay, that's right now; I thought there was something in *him*." "Bless me—such a story!" After this manner ran on her unconscious comments. She was a considerable politician, and this was an interesting debate; and you could very soon make out by her continual observations the political opinions of the mistress of Killiecrankie. She was a desperate Tory, and at the same moment the most direful and unconstitutional of Radicals. With a hereditary respect she applauded the sentiments of the old country-party, and clung to every institution with the pertinacity of a martyr; yet with the same breath, and the most delightful inconsistency, was vehement and enthusiastic in favour of the wildest schemes of reform; which, we suppose, is as much as to say that Miss Willsie was a very feminine politician, the most unreasonable of optimists, and had the sublimest contempt for all practical considerations when she had convinced herself that anything was *right*.

"I knew it!" cried Miss Willsie, with a burst of triumph; "he's out, and every one disowning him—a mean crew, big and little! If there's one thing I hate, it's setting a man forward to tell an untruth, and then letting him bear all the blame!"

"He's got his lawful deserts," said Mr Foggo. This gentleman, more learned than his sister, took a very philosophical view of public matters, and acknowledged no particular leaning to any "party" in his general interest in the affairs of state.

"I never can find out now," said Miss Willsie suddenly, "what the like of Mr Atheling can have to do with this man—a lord and a great person, and an officer of state—but his eye kindles up at the name of him, as if it was the name of a friend. There cannot be ill-will unless there is acquaintance, that's my opinion; and an ill-will at this lord I am sure Mr Atheling has."

"They come from the same countryside," said Mr Foggo; "when they were lads they knew each other."

"And who is this Mr Atheling?" said Endicott, speaking for the first time. "I have a letter of introduction to Viscount Winterbourne myself. His son, the Honourable George Rivers, travelled in the States a year or two since, and I mean to see him by-and-by; but who is Mr Atheling, to know an English Secretary of State?"

"He's Cash and Ledger's chief clerk," said Mr Foggo, very laconically, looking with a steady eye at the candlestick, and bestowing as little attention upon his questioner as his questioner did upon him.

"Marvellous! in this country!" said the American; but Mr Endicott belonged to that young America which is mightily respectful of the old country. He thought it vulgar to do too much republicanism. He only heightened the zest of his admiration now and then by a refined little sneer.

"In this country! Where did ye ever see such a country, I would like to know?" cried Miss Willsie. "If it was but for your own small concerns, you ought to be thankful; for London itself will keep ye in writing this many a day. If there's one thing I cannot bear, it's ingratitude! I'm a long-suffering person myself; but that, I grant, gets the better of me."

"Mr Atheling, I suppose, has not many lords in his acquaintance," said Harry Oswald, looking up from his paper. "Endicott is right enough, aunt; he is not quite in the rank for that; he has better——" said Harry, something lowering his voice; "I would rather know myself welcome at the Athelings' than in any other house in England."

This was said with a little enthusiasm, and brought the rising colour to Harry Oswald's brow. His cousin looked at him, with a curl of his thin lip and a somewhat malignant eye. Miss Willsie looked at him hastily, with a quick impatient nod of her head, and a most rapid and emphatic frown. Finally, Mr Foggo lifted to the young man's face his acute and steady eye.

"Keep to your physic, Harry," said Mr Foggo. The hapless Harry did not meet the glance, but he understood the tone.

"Well, uncle, well," said Harry hastily, raising his eyes; "but a man cannot always keep to physic. There are more things in the world than drugs and lancets. A man must have some margin for his thoughts."

Again Miss Willsie gave the culprit a nod and a frown, saying as plain as telegraphic communication ever said, "I am your friend, but this is not the time to plead." Again Mr Endicott surveyed his cousin with a vague impulse of malice and of rivalry. Harry Oswald plunged down again on his paper, and was no more heard of that night.

CHAPTER XV
THE PROPOSAL

"I suppose we are not going to hear anything about it. It is very hard," said Agnes disconsolately. "I am sure it is so easy to show a little courtesy. Mr Burlington surely might have written to let us know."

"But, my dear, how can we tell?" said Mrs Atheling; "he may be ill, or he may be out of town, or he may have trouble in his family. It is very difficult to judge another person—and you don't know what may have happened; he may be coming here himself, for aught we know."

"Well, I think it is very hard," said Marian; "I wish we only could publish it ourselves. What is the good of a publisher? They are only cruel to everybody, and grow rich themselves; it is always so in books."

"He might surely have written at least," repeated Agnes. These young malcontents were extremely dissatisfied, and not at all content with Mrs Atheling's explanation that he might be ill, or out of town, or have trouble in his family. Whatever extenuating circumstances there might be, it was clear that Mr Burlington had not behaved properly, or with the regard for other people's feelings which Agnes concluded to be the only true mark of a gentleman. Even the conversation of last night, and the state and greatness of Mr Endicott, stimulated the impatience of the girls. "It is not for the book so much, as for the uncertainty," Agnes said, as she disconsolately took out her sewing; but in fact it was just because they had so much certainty, and so little change and commotion in their life, that they longed so much for the excitement and novelty of this new event.

They were very dull this afternoon, and everything out of doors sympathised with their dulness. It was a wet day—a hopeless, heavy, persevering, not-to-be-mended day of rain. The clouds hung low and leaden over the wet world; the air was clogged and dull with moisture, only lightened now and then by an impatient shrewish gust, which threw the small raindrops like so many prickles full into your face. The long branches of the lilacs blew about wildly with a sudden commotion, when one of these gusts came upon them, like a group of heroines throwing up their arms in a tragic appeal to heaven. The primroses, pale and drooping, sullied their cheeks with the wet soil; hour after hour, with the most sullen and dismal obstinacy, the rain rained down upon the cowering earth; not a sound was in Bellevue save the trickle of the water, a perfect stream, running strong and full down the little channel on either side the street. It was in vain to go to the window, where not a single passenger—not a baker's boy, nor a maid on pattens, nobody but the milkman in his waterproof-coat—hurrying along, a peripatetic fountain, with little jets of water pouring from his hat, his cape, and his pails—was visible through the whole dreary afternoon. It is possible to endure a wet morning—easy enough to put up with a wet night; but they must have indeed high spirits and pleasurable occupations who manage to keep their patience and their cheerfulness through the sullen and dogged monotony of a wet afternoon.

So everybody had a poke at the fire, which had gone out twice to-day already, and was maliciously looking for another opportunity of going out again; every person here present snapped her thread and lost her needle; every one, even, each for a single moment, found Bell and Beau in her way. You may suppose, this being the case, how very dismal the circumstances must have been. But suddenly everybody started—the outer gate swung open—an audible footstep came towards the door! Fairest of readers, a word with you! If you are given to morning-calls, and love to be welcomed, make your visits on a wet day!

It was not a visitor, however welcome—better than that—ecstatic sound! it was the postman—the postman, drenched and sullen, hiding his crimson glories under an oilskin cape; and it was a letter, solemn and mysterious, in an unknown hand—a big blue letter, addressed to Miss Atheling. With trembling fingers Agnes opened it, taking, with awe and apprehension, out of the big blue envelope, a blue and big enclosure and a little note. The paper fell to the ground, and was seized upon by Marian. The excited girl sprang up with it, almost upsetting Bell and Beau. "It is in print! Memorandum of an agreement—oh, mamma!" cried Marian, holding up the dangerous instrument. Agnes sat down immediately in her chair, quite hushed for the instant. It was an actual reality, Mr Burlington's letter—and a veritable proposal—not for herself, but for her book.

The girls, we are obliged to confess, were slightly out of their wits for about an hour after this memorable arrival. Even Mrs Atheling was excited, and Bell and Beau ran about the room in unwitting exhilaration, shouting at the top of their small sweet shrill voices, and tumbling over each other unreproved. The good mother, to tell the truth, would have liked to cry a little, if she could have managed it, and was much moved, and disposed to take this, not as a mere matter of business, but as a tender office of friendship and esteem on the part of the unconscious Mr Burlington. Mrs Atheling could not help fancying that somehow this wonderful chance had happened to Agnes because she was "a good girl."

And until Papa and Charlie came home they were not very particular about the conditions of the agreement; the event itself was the thing which moved them: it quickened the slow pace of this dull afternoon to the most extraordinary celerity; the moments flew now which had lagged with such obstinate dreariness before the coming of that postman; and all the delight and astonishment of the first moment remained to be gone over again at the home-coming of Papa.

And Mr Atheling, good man, was almost as much disturbed for the moment as his wife. At first he was incredulous—then he laughed, but the laugh was extremely unsteady in its sound—then he read over the paper with great care, steadily resisting the constant interruptions of Agnes and Marian, who persecuted him with their questions, "What do you think of it, papa?" before the excellent papa had time to think at all. Finally, Mr Atheling laughed again with more composure, and spread out upon the table the important "Memorandum of Agreement." "Sign it, Agnes," said Papa; "it seems all right, and quite business-like, so far as I can see. She's not twenty-one, yet—I don't suppose it's legal—that child! Sign it, Agnes."

This was by no means what Papa was expected to say; yet Agnes, with excitement, got her blotting-book and her pen. This innocent family were as anxious that Agnes's autograph should be *well written* as if it had been intended for a specimen of caligraphy, instead of the signature to a legal document; nor was the young author herself less concerned; and she made sure of the pen, and steadied her hand conscientiously before she wrote that pretty "Agnes Atheling," which put the other ugly printer-like handwriting completely to shame. And now it was done—there was a momentary pause of solemn silence, not disturbed even by Bell and Beau.

"So this is the beginning of Agnes's fortune," said Mr Atheling. "Now Mary, and all of you, don't be excited; every book does not succeed because it finds a publisher; and you must not place your expectations too high; for you know Agnes knows nothing of the world."

It was very good to say "don't be excited," when Mr Atheling himself was entirely oblivious of his newspaper, indifferent to his tea, and actually did not hear the familiar knock of Mr Foggo at the outer door.

"And these half profits, papa, I wonder what they will be," said Agnes, glad to take up something tangible in this vague delight.

"Oh, something very considerable," said Papa, forgetting his own caution. "I should not wonder if the publisher made a great deal of money by it: *they* know what they're about. Get up and get me my slippers, you little rascals. When Agnes comes into her fortune, what a paradise of toys for Bell and Beau!"

But the door opened, and Mr Foggo came in like a big brown cloud. There was no concealing from him the printed paper—no hiding the overflowings of the family content. So Agnes and Marian hurried off for half an hour's practising, and then put the twins to bed, and gossiped over the fire in the little nursery. What a pleasant night it was!

CHAPTER XVI
FAMILY EXCITEMENT

It would be impossible to describe, after that first beginning, the pleasant interest and excitement kept up in this family concerning the fortune of Agnes. All kinds of vague and delightful magnificences floated in the minds of the two girls: guesses of prodigious sums of money and unimaginable honours were constantly hazarded by Marian; and Agnes, though she laughed at, and professed to disbelieve, these splendid imaginations, was, beyond all controversy, greatly influenced by them. The house held up its head, and began to dream of fame and greatness. Even Mr Atheling, in a trance of exalted and exulting fancy, went down self-absorbed through the busy moving streets, and scarcely noticed the steady current of the Islingtonian public setting in strong for the City. Even Mamma, going about her household business, had something visionary in her eye; she saw a long way beyond to-day's little cares and difficulties—the grand distant lights of the future streaming down on the fair heads of her two girls. It was not possible, at least in the mother's fancy, to separate these two who were so closely united. No one in the house, indeed, could recognise Agnes without Marian, or Marian without Agnes; and this new fortune belonged to both.

And then there followed all those indefinite but glorious adjuncts involved in this beginning of fate—society, friends, a class of people, as those good dreamers supposed, more able to understand and appreciate the simple and modest refinement of these young minds;—all the world was to be moved by this one book—everybody was to render homage—all society to be disturbed with eagerness. Mr Atheling adjured the family not to raise their expectations too high, yet raised his own to the most magnificent level of unlikely greatness. Mrs Atheling had generous compunctions of mind as she looked at the ribbons already half faded. Agnes now was in a very different position from her who made the unthrifty purchase of a colour which would not bear the sun. Mamma held a very solemn synod in her own mind, and was half resolved to buy new ones upon her own responsibility. But then there was something shabby in building upon an expectation which as yet was so indefinite. And we are glad to say there was so much sobriety and good sense in the house of the Athelings, despite their glorious anticipations, that the ribbons of Agnes and Marian, though they began to fulfil Mrs Atheling's prediction, still steadily did their duty, and bade fair to last out their appointed time.

This was a very pleasant time to the whole household. Their position, their comfort, their external circumstances, were in no respect changed, yet everything was brightened and radiant in an overflow of hope. There was neither ill nor sickness nor sorrow to mar the enjoyment; everything at this period was going well with them, to whom many a day and many a year had gone full heavily. They were not aware themselves of their present happiness; they were all looking eagerly forward, bent upon a future which was to be so much superior to to-day, and none dreamed how little pleasure was to be got out of the realisation, in comparison with the delight they all took in the hope. They could afford so well to laugh at all their homely difficulties—to make jokes upon Mamma's grave looks as she discovered an extravagant shilling or two in the household accounts—or found out that Susan had been wasteful in the kitchen. It was so odd, so *funny*, to contrast these minute cares with the golden age which was to come.

And then the plans and secret intentions, the wonderful committees which sat in profound retirement; Marian plotting with Mamma what Agnes should have when she came into her fortune, and Agnes advising, with the same infallible authority, for the advantage of Marian. The vast and ambitious project of the girls for going to the country—the country or the sea-side—some one, they did not care which, of those beautiful unknown beatific regions out of London, which were to them all fairyland and countries of magic. We suppose nobody ever did enjoy the sea breezes as Agnes and Marian Atheling, in their little white bed-chamber, enjoyed the imaginary gale upon the imaginary sands, which they could perceive brightening the cheek of Mamma, and tossing about the curls of the twin-babies, at any moment of any night or day. This was to be the grand triumph of the time when Agnes came into her fortune, though even Mamma as yet had not heard of the project; but already it was a greater pleasure to the girls than any real visit to any real sea-side in this visible earth ever could be.

And then there began to come, dropping in at all hours, from the earliest post in the morning to the last startling delivery at nine o'clock at night, packets of printed papers—the proof-sheets of this astonishing book. You are not to suppose that those proofs needed much correcting—Agnes's manuscript was far too daintily written for that; yet every one read them with the utmost care and attention, and Papa made little crosses in pencil on the margin when he came to a doubtful word. Everybody read them, not once only, but sometimes twice, or even three times over—everybody but Charlie, who eat them up with his bread and butter at tea, did not say a word on the subject, and never looked at them again. All Bellevue resounded with the knocks of that incessant postman at Number Ten. Public opinion was divided on the subject. Some people said the Athelings had been extravagant, and were now suffering under a very Egyptian plague, a hailstorm of bills; others, more charitable, had private information that both the Miss Athelings were going to be married, and believed this continual dropping to be a carnival shower of flowers and *bonbons*, the love-letters of the affianced bridegrooms; but nobody supposed that the unconscious and innocent postman stood a respectable deputy for the little Beelzebub, to whose sooty hands of natural right should have been committed the custody of those fair and uncorrectable sheets. Sometimes, indeed, this sable emissary made a hasty and half-visible appearance in his own proper person, with one startling knock, as loud, but more solemn than the postman—"That's the Devil!" said Charlie, with unexpected animation, the second time this emphatic sound was heard; and Susan refused point-blank to open the door.

How carefully these sheets were corrected! how punctually they were returned!—with what conscientious care and earnestness the young author attended to all the requirements of printer and publisher! There was something amusing, yet something touching as well, in the sincere and natural humbleness of these simple people. Whatever they said, they could not help thinking that some secret spring of kindness had moved Mr Burlington; that somehow this unconscious gentleman, most innocent of any such intention, meant to do them all a favour. And moved by the influence of this amiable delusion, Agnes was scrupulously attentive to all the suggestions of the publisher. Mr Burlington himself was somewhat amused by his new writer's obedience, but doubtful, and did not half understand it; for it is not always easy to comprehend downright and simple sincerity. But the young author went on upon her guileless way, taking no particular thought of her own motives; and on with her every step went all the family, excited and unanimous. To her belonged the special joy of being the cause of this happy commotion; but the pleasure and the honour and the delight belonged equally to them all.

CHAPTER XVII
AN AMERICAN SKETCH

"Here! there's reading for you," said Miss Willsie, throwing upon the family table a little roll of papers. "They tell me there's something of the kind stirring among yourselves. If there's one thing I cannot put up with, it's to see a parcel of young folk setting up to read lessons to the world!"

"Not Agnes!" cried Marian eagerly; "only wait till it comes out. I know so well, Miss Willsie, how you will like her book."

"No such thing," said Miss Willsie indignantly. "I would just like to know—twenty years old, and never out of her mother's charge a week at a time—I would just like any person to tell me what Agnes Atheling can have to say to the like of me!"

"Indeed, nothing at all," said Agnes, blushing and laughing; "but it is different with Mr Endicott. Now nobody must speak a word. Here it is."

"No! let me away first," cried Miss Willsie in terror. She was rather abrupt in her exits and entrances. This time she disappeared instantaneously, shaking her hand at some imaginary culprit, and had closed the gate behind her with a swing, before Agnes was able to begin the series of "Letters from England" which were to immortalise the name of Mr Foggo S. Endicott. The New World biographist began with his voyage, and all the "emotions awakened in his breast" by finding himself at sea; and immediately thereafter followed a special chapter, headed "Killiecrankie Lodge."

"How delightful," wrote the traveller, "so many thousand miles from home, so far away from those who love us, to meet with the sympathy and communion of kindred blood! To this home of the domestic affections I am glad at once to introduce my readers, as a beautiful example of that Old England felicity, which is, I grieve to say, so sadly outbalanced by oppression and tyranny and crime! This beautiful suburban retreat is the home of my respected relatives, Mr F. and his maiden sister Miss Wilhelmina F. Here they live with old books, old furniture, and old pictures around them, with old plate upon their table, old servants in waiting, and an old cat coiled up in comfort upon their cosy hearth! A graceful air of antiquity pervades everything. The inkstand from which I write belonged to a great-grandfather; the footstool under my feet was worked by an old lady of the days of the lovely Queen Mary; and I cannot define the date of the china in that carved cabinet: all this, which would be out of place in one of the splendid palaces of our buzy citizens, is here in perfect harmony with the character of the inmates. It is such a house as naturally belongs to an old country, an old family, and an old and secluded pair.

"My uncle is an epitome of all that is worthy in man. Like most remarkable Scotsmen, he takes snuff; and to perceive his penetration and wise sagacity, one has only to look at the noble head which he carries with a hereditary loftiness. His sister is a noble old lady, and entirely devoted to him. In fact, they are all the world to each other; and the confidence with which the brother confides all his cares and sorrows to the faithful bosom of his sister, is a truly touching sight; while Miss Wilhelmina F., on her part, seldom makes an observation without winding up by a reference to 'my brother.' It is a long time since I have found anywhere so fresh and delightful an object of study as the different characteristics of this united pair. It is beautiful to watch the natural traits unfolding themselves. One has almost as much pleasure in the investigation as one has in studying the developments of childhood; and my admirable relatives are as delightfully unconscious of their own distinguishing qualities as even children could be.

"Their house is a beautiful little suburban villa, far from the noise and din of the great city. Here they spend their beautiful old age in hospitality and beneficence; beggars (for there are always beggars in England) come to the door every morning with patriarchal familiarity, and receive their dole through an opening in the door, like the ancient buttery-hatch; every morning, upon the garden paths crumbs are strewed for the robins and the sparrows, and the birds come hopping fearlessly about the old lady's feet, trusting in her gracious nature. All the borders are filled with wallflowers, the favourite plant of Miss Wilhelmina, and they seemed to me to send up a sweeter fragrance when she watered them with her delicate little engine, or pruned them with her own hand; for everything, animate and inanimate, seems to know that she is good.

"To complete this delightful picture, there is just that shade of solicitude and anxiety wanting to make it perfect. They have a nephew, this excellent couple, over whom they watch with the characteristic jealousy of age watching youth. While my admirable uncle eats his egg at breakfast, he talks of Harry; while aunt Wilhelmina pours out the tea from her magnificent old silver teapot, she makes apologies and excuses for him. They will make him their heir, I do not doubt, for he is a handsome and prepossessing youth; and however this may be to *my* injury, I joyfully waive my claim; for the sight of their tender affection and beautiful solicitude is a greater boon to a student of mankind like myself than all their old hereditary hoards or patrimonial acres; and so I say, Good fortune to Harry, and let all my readers say Amen!"

We are afraid to say how difficult Agnes found it to accomplish this reading in peace; but in spite of Marian's laughter and Mrs Atheling's indignant interruptions, Agnes herself was slightly impressed by these fine sentiments and pretty sentences. She laid down the paper with an air of extreme perplexity, and could scarcely be tempted to smile. "Perhaps that is how Mr Endicott sees things," said Agnes; "perhaps he has so fine a mind—perhaps—Now, I am sure, mamma, if you had not known Miss Willsie, you would have thought it very pretty. I know you would."

"Do not speak to me, child," cried Mrs Atheling energetically. "Pretty! why, he is coming here to-night!"

And Marian clapped her hands. "Mamma will be in the next one!" cried Marian; "and he will find out that Agnes is a great author, and that we are all so anxious about Charlie. Oh, I hope he will send us a copy. What fun it would be to read about papa and his newspaper, and what everybody was doing at home here in Bellevue!"

"It would be very impertinent," said Mrs Atheling, reddening with anger; "and if anything of the kind should happen, I will never forgive Mr Foggo. You will take care to speak as little as possible to him, Marian; he is not a safe person. Pretty! Does he think he has a right to come into respectable houses and make his pretty pictures? You must be very much upon your guard, girls. I forbid you to be friendly with such a person as *that*!"

"But perhaps"—said Agnes.

"Perhaps—nonsense," cried Mamma indignantly; "he must not come in here, that I am resolved. Go and tell Susan we will sit in the best room to-night."

But Agnes meditated the matter anxiously—perhaps, though she did not say it—perhaps to be a great literary personage, it was necessary to "find good in everything," after the newest fashion, like Mr Endicott. Agnes was much puzzled, and somewhat discouraged, on her own account. She did not think it possible she could ever come to such a sublime and elevated view of ordinary things; she felt herself a woeful way behind Mr Endicott, and with a little eagerness looked forward to his visit. Would he justify himself—what would he say?

CHAPTER XVIII
COMPANY

The best room was not by any means so bright, so cheerful, or so kindly as the family parlour, with its family disarrangement, and the amateur paperhanging upon its walls. Before their guests arrived the girls made an effort to improve its appearance. They pulled the last beautiful bunches of the lilac to fill the little glass vases, and placed candles in the ornamental glass candlesticks upon the mantelpiece. But even a double quantity of light did not bring good cheer to this dull and solemn apartment. Had it been winter, indeed, a fire might have made a difference; but it was early summer—one of those balmy nights so sweet out of doors, which give an additional shade of gloom to dark-complexioned parlours, shutting out the moon and the stars, the night air and the dew. Agnes and Marian, fanciful and visionary, kept the door open themselves, and went wandering about the dark garden, where the summer flowers came slowly, and the last primrose was dying pale and sweet under the poplar tree. They went silently and singly, one after the other, through the garden paths, hearing, without observing, the two different footsteps which came to the front door. If they were thinking, neither of them knew or could tell what she was thinking about, and they returned to the house without a word, only knowing how much more pleasant it was to be out here in the musical and breathing darkness, than to be shut closely within the solemn enclosure of the best room.

But there, by the table where Marian had maliciously laid his paper, was the stately appearance of Mr Endicott, holding high his abstracted head, while Harry Oswald, anxious, and yet hesitating, lingered at the door, eagerly on the watch for the light step of which he had so immediate a perception when it came. Harry, who indeed had no great inducement to be much in love with himself, forgot himself altogether as his quick ear listened for the foot of Marian. Mr Endicott, on the contrary, added a loftier shape to his abstraction, by way of attracting and not expressing admiration. Unlucky Harry was in love with Marian; his intellectual cousin only aimed at making Marian in love with *him*.

And she came in, slightly conscious, we admit, that she was the heroine of the night, half aware of the rising rivalry, half-enlightened as to the different character of these two very different people, and of the one motive which brought them here. So a flitting changeable blush went and came upon the face of Marian. Her eyes, full of the sweet darkness and dew of the night, were dazzled by the lights, and would not look steadily at any one; yet a certain gleam of secret mischief and amusement in her face betrayed itself to Harry Oswald, though not at all to the unsuspicious American. She took her seat very sedately at the table, and busied herself with her fancy-work. Mr Endicott sat opposite, looking at her; and Harry, a moving shadow in the dim room, hovered about, sitting and standing behind her chair.

Besides these young people, Mr Atheling, Mr Foggo, and Mamma, were in the room, conversing among themselves, and taking very little notice of the other visitors. Mamma was making a little frock, upon which she bestowed unusual pains, as it seemed; for no civility of Mr Endicott could gain any answer beyond a monosyllable from the virtuous and indignant mistress of the house. He was playing with his own papers as Agnes and Marian came to the table, affectionately turning them over, and looking at the heading of the "Letter from England" with a loving eye.

"You are interested in literature, I believe?" said Mr Endicott. Agnes, Marian, and Harry, all of them glancing at him in the same moment, could not tell which he addressed; so there was a confused murmur of reply. "Not in the slightest," cried Harry Oswald, behind Marian's chair. "Oh, but Agnes is!" cried Marian; and Agnes herself, with a conscious blush, acknowledged—"Yes, indeed, very much."

"But not, I suppose, very well acquainted with the American press?" said Mr Endicott. "The bigotry of Europeans is marvellous. We read your leading papers in the States, but I have not met half-a-dozen people in England—actually not six individuals—who were in the frequent habit of seeing the *Mississippi Gazette*."

"We rarely see any newspapers at all," said Agnes, apologetically. "Papa has his paper in the evenings, but except now and then, when there is a review of a book in it——"

"That is the great want of English contemporary literature," interrupted Mr Endicott. "You read the review—good! but you feel that something else is wanted than mere politics—that votes and debates do not supply the wants of the age!"

"If the wants of the age were the wants of young ladies," said Harry Oswald, "what would become of my uncle and Mr Atheling? Leave things in their proper place, Endicott. Agnes and Marian want something different from newspaper literature and leading articles. Don't interfere with the girls."

"These are the slavish and confined ideas of a worn out civilisation," said the man of letters; "in my country we respect the opinions of our women, and give them full scope."

"Respect!—the old humbug!" muttered Harry behind Marian's chair. "Am I disrespectful? I choose to be judged by you."

Marian glanced over her shoulder with saucy kindness. "Don't quarrel," said Marian. No! Poor Harry was so glad of the glance, the smile, and the confidence, that he could have taken Endicott, who was the cause of it, to his very heart.

"The functions of the press," said Mr Endicott, "are unjustly limited in this country, like most other enlightened influences. In these days we have scarcely time to wait for books. It is not with us as it was in old times, when the soul lay fallow for a century, and then blossomed into its glorious epic, or drama, or song! Our audience must perceive the visible march of mind, hour by hour and day by day. We are no longer concerned about mere physical commotions, elections, or debates, or votes of the Senate. In these days we care little for the man's opinions; what we want is an advantageous medium for studying the man."

As she listened to this, Agnes Atheling held her breath, and suspended her work unawares. It sounded very imposing, indeed—to tell the truth, it sounded something like that magnificent conversation in books over which Marian and she had often marvelled. Then this simple girl believed in everybody; she was rather inclined to suppose of Mr Endicott that he was a man of very exalted mind.

"I do not quite know," said Agnes humbly, "whether it is right to tell all about great people in the newspapers, or even to put them in books. Do you think it is, Mr Endicott?"

"I think," said the American, solemnly, "that a public man, and, above all, a literary man, belongs to the world. All the exciting scenes of life come to us only that we may describe and analyse them for the advantage of others. A man of genius has no private life. Of what benefit is the keenness of his emotions if he makes no record of them? In my own career," continued the literary gentleman, "I have been sometimes annoyed by foolish objections to the notice I am in the habit of giving of friends who cross my way. Unenlightened people have complained of me, in vulgar phrase, that I 'put them in the newspapers.' How strange a misconception! for you must perceive at once that it was not with any consideration of them, but simply that my readers might see every scene I passed through, and in reality feel themselves travelling with *me*!"

"Oh!" Agnes made a faint and very doubtful exclamation; Harry Oswald turned on his heel, and left the room abruptly; while Marian bent very closely over her work, to conceal that she was laughing. Mr Endicott thought it was a natural youthful reverence, and gave her all due credit for her "ingenuous emotions."

"The path of genius necessarily reveals certain obscure individuals," said Mr Endicott; "they cross its light, and the poet has no choice. I present to my audience the scenes through which I travel. I introduce the passengers on the road. Is it for the sake of these passengers? No. It is that my readers may be enabled, under all circumstances, to form a just realisation of *me*. That is the true vocation of a poet: he ought to be in himself the highest example of everything—joy, delight, suffering, remorse, and ruin—yes, I am bold enough to say, even crime. No man should be able to suppose that he can hide himself in an indescribable region of emotion where the poet cannot follow. Shall murder be permitted to attain an experience beyond the reach of genius? No! Everything must be possessed by the poet's intuitions, for he himself is the great lesson of the world."

"Charlie," said Harry Oswald behind the door, "come in, and punch this fellow's head."

CHAPTER XIX
CONVERSATION

Charlie came in, but not to punch the head of Mr Endicott. The big boy gloomed upon the dignified American, pushed Harry Oswald aside, and brought his two grammars to the table. "I say, what do you want with me?" said Charlie; he was not at all pleased at having been disturbed.

"Nobody wanted you, Charlie,—no one ever wants you, you disagreeable boy," said Marian: "it was all Harry Oswald's fault; he thought we were too pleasant all by ourselves here."

To which complimentary saying Mr Endicott answered by a bow. He quite understood what Miss Marian meant! he was much flattered to have gained her sympathy! So Marian pleased both her admirers for once, for Harry Oswald laughed in secret triumph behind her chair.

"And you are still with Mr Bell, Harry," said Mrs Atheling, suddenly interposing. "I am very glad you like this place—and what a pleasure it must be to all your sisters! I begin to think you are quite settled now."

"I suppose it was time," said Harry the unlucky, colouring a little, but smiling more as he came out from the shadow of Marian's chair, in compliment to Marian's mother; "yes, we get on very well,—we are not overpowered with our practice; so much the better for me."

"But you ought to be more ambitious,—you ought to try to extend your practice," said Mrs Atheling, immediately falling into the tone of an adviser, in addressing one to whom everybody gave good advice.

"I might have some comfort in it, if I was a poet," said Harry; "but to kill people simply in the way of business is too much for me.—Well, uncle, it is no fault of mine. I never did any honour to my doctorship. I am as well content to throw physic to the dogs as any Macbeth in the world."

"Ay, Harry," said Mr Foggo; "but I think it is little credit to a man to avow ill inclinations, unless he has the spirit of a man to make head against them. That's my opinion—but I know you give it little weight."

"A curious study!" said Mr Endicott, reflectively. "I have watched it many times,—the most interesting conflict in the world."

But Harry, who had borne his uncle's reproof with calmness, reddened fiercely at this, and seemed about to resent it. The study of character, though it is so interesting a study, and so much pursued by superior minds, is not, as a general principle, at all liked by the objects of it. Harry Oswald, under the eye of his cousin's curious inspection, had the greatest mind in the world to knock that cousin down.

"And what do you think of our domestic politics, on the other side of the Atlantic?" asked Papa, joining the more general conversation: "a pretty set of fellows manage us in Old England here. I never take up a newspaper but there's a new job in it. If it were only for other countries, they might have a sense of shame!"

"Well, sir," said Mr Endicott, "considering all things—considering the worn-out circumstances of the old country, your oligarchy and your subserviency, I am rather disposed, on the whole, to be in favour of the government of England. So far as a limited intelligence goes, they really appear to me to get on pretty well."

"Humph!" said Mr Atheling. He was quite prepared for a dashing republican denunciation, but this cool patronage stunned the humble politician—he did not comprehend it. "However," he continued, reviving after a little, and rising into triumph, "there is principle among them yet. They cannot tolerate a man who wants the English virtue of keeping his word; no honourable man will keep office with a traitor. Winterbourne's out. There's some hope for the country when one knows that."

"And who is Winterbourne, papa?" asked Agnes, who was near her father.

Mr Atheling was startled. "Who is Lord Winterbourne, child? why, a disgraced minister—everybody knows!"

"You speak as if you were glad," said Agnes, possessed with a perfectly unreasonable pertinacity: "do you know him, papa,—has he done anything to you?"

"I!" cried Mr Atheling, "how should I know him? There! thread your needle, and don't ask ridiculous questions. Lord Winterbourne for himself is of no consequence to me."

From which everybody present understood immediately that this unknown personage *was* of consequence to Mr Atheling—that Papa certainly knew him, and that he had "done something" to call for so great an amount of virtuous indignation. Even Mr Endicott paused in the little account he proposed to give of Viscount Winterbourne's title and acquirements, and his own acquaintance with the Honourable George Rivers, his lordship's only son. A vision of family feuds and mysteries crossed the active mind of the American: he stopped to make a mental note of this interesting circumstance; for Mr Endicott did not disdain to embellish his "letters" now and then with a fanciful legend, and this was certainly "suggestive" in the highest degree.

"I remember," said Mrs Atheling, suddenly, "when we were first married, we went to visit an old aunt of papa's, who lived quite close to Winterbourne Hall. Do you remember old Aunt Bridget, William? We have not heard anything of her for many a day; she lived in an old house, half made of timber, and ruinous with ivy. I remember it very well; I thought it quite pretty when I was a girl."

"Ruinous! you mean beautiful with ivy, mamma," said Marian.

"No, my dear; ivy is a very troublesome thing," said Mrs Atheling, "and makes a very damp house, I assure you, though it looks pretty. This was just upon the edge of a wood, and on a hill. There was a very fine view from it; all the spires, and domes, and towers looked beautiful with the morning sun upon them. I suppose Aunt Bridget must still be living, William? I wonder why she took offence at us. What a pleasant place that would have been to take the children in summer! It was called the Old Wood Lodge, and there was a larger place near which was the Old Wood House, and the nearest house to that, I believe, was the Hall. It was a very pretty place; I remember it so well."

Agnes and Marian exchanged glances; this description was quite enough to set their young imaginations a-glow;—perhaps, for the sake of her old recollections, Mamma would like this better than the sea-side.

"Should you like to go again, mamma?" said Agnes, in a half whisper. Mamma smiled, and brightened, and shook her head.

"No, my dear, no; you must not think of such a thing—travelling is so very expensive," said Mrs Atheling; but the colour warmed and brightened on her cheek with pleasure at the thought.

"And of course there's another family of children," said Papa, in a somewhat sullen under-tone. "Aunt Bridget, when she dies, will leave the cottage to one of them. They always wanted it. Yes, to be sure,—to him that hath shall be given,—it is the way of the world."

"William, William; you forget what you say!" cried Mrs Atheling, in alarm.

"I mean no harm, Mary," said Papa, "and the words bear that meaning as well as another: it is the way of the world."

"Had I known your interest in the family, I might have brought you some information," interposed Mr Endicott. "I have a letter of introduction to Viscount Winterbourne—and saw a great deal of the Honourable George Rivers when he travelled in the States."

"I have no interest in them—not the slightest," said Mr Atheling, hastily; and Harry Oswald moved away from where he had been standing to resume his place by Marian, a proceeding which instantly distracted the attention of his cousin and rival. The girls were talking to each other of this new imaginary paradise. Harry Oswald could not explain how it was, but he began immediately with all his skill to make a ridiculous picture of the old house, which was half made of timber, and ruinous with ivy: he could not make out why he listened with such a jealous pang to the very name of this Old Wood Lodge.

CHAPTER XX
AUNT BRIDGET

"Very strange!" said Mr Atheling—he had just laid upon the breakfast-table a letter edged with black, which had startled them all for the moment into anxiety,—"very strange!"

"What is very strange?—who is it, William?" asked Mrs Atheling, anxiously.

"Do you remember how you spoke of her last night?—only last night—my Aunt Bridget, of whom we have not heard for years? I could almost be superstitious about this," said Papa. "Poor old lady! she is gone at last."

Mrs Atheling read the letter eagerly. "And she spoke of us, then?—she was sorry. Who could have persuaded her against us, William?" said the good mother—"and wished you should attend her funeral. You will go?—surely you must go." But as she spoke, Mrs Atheling paused and considered—travelling is not so easy a matter, when people have only two hundred a-year.

"It would do her no pleasure now, Mary," said Mr Atheling, with a momentary sadness. "Poor Aunt Bridget; she was the last of all the old generation; and now it begins to be our turn."

In the mean time, however, it was time for the respectable man of business to be on his way to his office. His wife brushed his hat with gravity, thinking upon his words. The old old woman who was gone, had left no responsibility behind her; but these children!—how could the father and the mother venture to die, and leave these young ones in the unfriendly world!

Charlie had gone to his office an hour ago—other studies, heavier and more discouraging even than the grammars, lay in the big law-books of Mr Foggo's office, to be conquered by this big boy. Throughout the day he had all the miscellaneous occupations which generally fall to the lot of the youngest clerk. Charlie said nothing about it to any one, but went in at these ponderous tomes in the morning. They were frightfully tough reading, and he was not given to literature; he shook his great fist at them, his natural enemies, and went in and conquered. These studies were pure pugilism so far as Charlie was concerned: he knocked down his ponderous opponent, mastered him, stowed away all his wisdom in his own prodigious memory, and replaced him on his shelf with triumph. "Now that old fellow's done for," said Charlie—and next morning the young student "went in" at the next.

Agnes and Marian were partly in this secret, as they had been in the previous one; so these young ladies came down stairs at seven o'clock to make breakfast for Charlie. It was nine now, and the long morning began to merge into the ordinary day; but the girls arrested Mamma on the threshold of her daily business to make eager inquiry about the Aunt Bridget, of whom, the only one among all their relatives, they knew little but the name.

"My dears, this is not a time to ask me," said Mrs Atheling: "there is Susan waiting, and there is the baker and the butterman at the door. Well, then, if you must know, she was just simply an old lady, and your grandpapa's sister; and she was once governess to Miss Rivers, and they gave her the old Lodge when the young lady should have been married. They made her a present of it—at least the old lord did—and she lived there ever after. It had been once in your grandpapa's family. I do not know the rights of the story—you can ask about it some time from your papa; but Aunt Bridget took quite a dislike to us after we were married—I cannot tell you why; and since the time I went to the Old Wood Lodge to pay her a visit, when I was a bride, I have never heard a kind word from her, poor old lady, till to-day. Now, my dears, let me go; do you see the people waiting? I assure you that is all."

And that was all that could be learned about Aunt Bridget, save a few unimportant particulars gleaned from the long conversation concerning her, which the father and the mother, much moralising, fell into that night. These young people had the instinct of curiosity most healthily developed; they listened eagerly to every new particular—heard with emotion that she had once been a beauty, and incontinently wove a string of romances about the name of the aged and humble spinster; and then what a continual centre of fancy and inquiry was that Old Wood Lodge!

A few days passed, and Aunt Bridget began to fade from her temporary prominence in the household firmament. A more immediate interest possessed the mind of the family—the book was coming out! Prelusive little paragraphs in the papers, which these innocent people did not understand to be advertisements, warned the public of a new and original work of fiction by a new author, about to be brought out by Mr Burlington, and which was expected to make a sensation when it came. Even the known and visible advertisements themselves were read with a startling thrill of interest. *Hope Hazlewood, a History*—everybody concluded it was the most felicitous title in the world.

The book was coming out, and great was the excitement of the household heart. The book came out!—there it lay upon the table in the family parlour, six fair copies in shiny blue cloth, with its name in letters of gold. These Mr Burlington intended should be sent to influential friends: but the young author had no influential friends; so one copy was sent to Killiecrankie Lodge, to the utter amazement of Miss Willsie, and another was carefully despatched to an old friend in the country, who scarcely knew what literature was; then the family made a solemn pause, and waited. What would everybody say?

Saturday came, full of fate. They knew all the names of all those dread and magnificent guides of public opinion, the literary newspapers; and with an awed and trembling heart, the young author waited for their verdict. She was so young, however, and in reality so ignorant of what might be the real issue of this first step into the world, that Agnes had a certain pleasure in her trepidation, and, scarcely knowing what she expected, knew only that it was in the highest degree novel, amusing, and extraordinary that these sublime and lofty people should ever be tempted to notice her at all. It was still only a matter of excitement and curiosity and amusing oddness to them all. If the young adventurer had been a man, this would have been a solemn crisis, full of fate: it was even so to a woman, seeking her own independence; but Agnes Atheling was only a girl in the heart of her family, and, looking out with laughing eyes upon her fortune, smiled at fate.

It is Saturday—yes, Saturday afternoon, slowly darkening towards the twilight. Agnes and Marian at the window are eagerly looking out, Mamma glances over their bright heads with unmistakable impatience, Papa is palpably restless in his easy-chair. Here he comes on flying feet, that big messenger of fortune—crossing the whole breadth of Bellevue in two strides, with ever so many papers in his hands. "Oh, I wonder what they will say!" cries Marian, clasping her pretty fingers. Agnes, too breathless to speak, makes neither guess nor answer—and here he comes!

It is half dark, and scarcely possible to read these momentous papers. The young author presses close to the window with the uncut *Athenæum*. There is Papa, half-risen from his chair; there is Mamma anxiously contemplating her daughter's face; there is Marian, reading over her shoulder; and Charlie stands with his hat on in the shade, holding fast in his hand the other papers. "One at a time!" says Charlie. He knows what they are, the grim young ogre, but he will not say a word.

And Agnes begins to read aloud—reads a sentence or two, suddenly stops, laughs hurriedly. "Oh, I cannot read that—somebody else take it," cried Agnes, running a rapid eye down the page; her cheeks are tingling, her eyes overflowing, her heart beating so loud that she does not hear her own voice. And now it is Marian who presses close to the window and reads aloud. Well! after all, it is not a very astonishing paragraph; it is extremely condescending, and full of the kindest patronage; recognises many beauties—a great deal of talent; and flatteringly promises the young author that by-and-by she will do very well. The reading is received with delight and disappointment. Mrs Atheling is not quite pleased that the reviewer refuses entire perfection to *Hope Hazlewood*, but by-and-by even the good mother is reconciled. Who could the critic be?—innocent critic, witting nothing of the tumult of kindly and grateful feelings raised towards him in a moment! Mrs Atheling cannot help setting it down certainly that he must be some unknown friend.

The others come upon a cooled enthusiasm—nobody feels that they have said the first good word. Into the middle of this reading Susan suddenly interposes herself and the candles. What tell-tales these lights are! Papa and Mamma, both of them, look mighty dazzled and unsteady about the eyes, and Agnes's cheeks are burning crimson-deep, and she scarcely likes to look at any one. She is half ashamed in her innocence—half as much ashamed as if they had been love-letters detected and read aloud.

And then after a while they come to a grave pause, and look at each other. "I suppose, mamma, it is sure to succeed now," says Agnes, very timidly, shading her face with her hand, and glancing up under its cover; and Papa, with his voice somewhat shaken, says solemnly, "Children, Agnes's fortune has come to-night."

For it was so out of the way—so uncommon and unexpected a fortune, to their apprehension, that the father and the mother looked on with wonder and amazement, as if at something coming down, without any human interposition, clear out of the hand of Providence, and from the treasures of heaven.

Upon the Monday morning following, Mr Atheling had another letter. It was a time of great events, and the family audience were interested even about this. Papa looked startled and affected, and read it without saying a word; then it was handed to Mamma: but Mrs Atheling, more demonstrative, ran over it with a constant stream of comment and exclamation, and at last read the whole epistle aloud. It ran thus:—

"Dear Sir,—Being intrusted by your Aunt, Miss Bridget Atheling, with the custody of her will, drawn up about a month before her death, I have now to communicate to you, with much pleasure, the particulars of the same. The will was read by me, upon the day of the funeral, in presence of the Rev. Lionel Rivers, rector of the parish; Dr Marsh, Miss Bridget's medical attendant; and Mrs Hardwicke, her niece. You are of course aware that your aunt's annuity died with her. Her property consisted of a thousand pounds in the Three per Cents, a small cottage in the village of Winterbourne, three acres of land in the hundred of Badgeley, and the Old Wood Lodge.

"Miss Bridget has bequeathed her personal property, all except the two last items, to Mrs Susannah Hardwicke, her niece—the Old Wood Lodge and the piece of land she bequeaths to you, William Atheling, being part, as she says, 'of the original property of the family.' She leaves it to you 'as a token that she had now discovered the falseness of the accusations made to her, twenty years ago, against you, and desires you to keep and to hold it, whatever attempts may be made to dislodge you, and whatever it may cost.' A copy of the will, pursuant to her own directions, will be forwarded to you in a few days.

"As an old acquaintance, I gladly congratulate you upon this legacy; but I am obliged to tell you, as a friend, that the property is not of that value which could have been desired. The land, which is of inferior quality, is let for fifteen shillings an acre, and the house, I am sorry to say, is not in very good condition, is very unlikely to find a tenant, and would cost half as much as it is worth to put it in tolerable repair—besides which, it stands directly in the way of the Hall, and was, as I understand, a gift to Miss Bridget only, with power, on the part of the Winterbourne family, to reclaim after her death. Under these circumstances, I doubt if you will be allowed to retain possession; notwithstanding, I call your attention to the emphatic words of my late respected client, to which you will doubtless give their due weight.—I am, dear sir, faithfully yours,

"Fred. R. Lewis, Attorney."

"And what shall we do? If we were only able to keep it, William—such a thing for the children!" cried Mrs Atheling, scarcely pausing to take breath. "To think that the Old Wood Lodge should be really ours—how strange it is! But, William, who could possibly have made false accusations against *you*?"

"Only one man," said Mr Atheling, significantly. The girls listened with interest and astonishment. "Only one man."

"No, no, my dear—no, it could not be— —," cried his wife: "you must not think so, William—it is quite impossible. Poor Aunt Bridget! and so she found out the truth at last."

"It is easy to talk," said the head of the house, looking over his letter; "very easy to leave a bequest like this, which can bring nothing but difficulty and trouble. How am I 'to keep and to hold it, at whatever cost?' The old lady must have been crazy to think of such a thing: she had much better have given it to my Lord at once without making any noise about it; for what is the use of bringing a quarrel upon me?"

"But, papa, it is the old family property," said Agnes, eagerly.

"My dear child, you know nothing about it," said Papa. "Do you think I am able to begin a lawsuit on behalf of the old family property? How were we to repair this tumble-down old house, if it had been ours on the securest holding? but to go to law about it, and it ready to crumble over our ears, is rather too much for the credit of the family. No, no; nonsense, children; you must not think of it for a moment; and you, Mary, surely you must see what folly it is."

But Mamma would not see any folly in the matter; her feminine spirit was roused, and her maternal pride. "You may depend upon it, Aunt Bridget had some motive," said Mrs Atheling, with a little excitement, "and real property, William, would be such a great thing for the children. Money might be lost or spent; but property—land and a house. My dear, you ought to consider how important it is for the children's sake."

Mr Atheling shook his head. "You are unreasonable," said the family father, who knew very well that he was pretty sure to yield to them, reason or no—"as unreasonable as you can be. Do you suppose I am a landed proprietor, with that old crazy Lodge, and forty-five shillings a-year? Mary, Mary, you ought to know better. We could not repair it, I tell you, and we could not furnish it; and nobody would rent it from us. We should gain nothing but an enemy, and that is no great advantage for the children. I do not remember that Aunt Bridget was ever remarkable for good sense; and it was no such great thing, after all, to transfer her family quarrel to me."

"Oh, papa, the old family property, and the beautiful old house in the country, where we could go and live in the summer!" said Marian. "Agnes is to be rich—Agnes would be sure to want to go somewhere in the country. We could do all the repairs ourselves—and mamma likes the place. Papa, papa, you will never have the heart to let other people have it. I think I can see the place; we could all go down when Agnes comes to her fortune—and the country would be so good for Bell and Beau."

This, perhaps, was the most irresistible of arguments. The eyes of the father and mother fell simultaneously upon the twin babies. They were healthy imps as ever did credit to a suburban atmosphere—yet somehow both Papa and Mamma fancied that Bell and Beau looked pale to-day.

"It is ten minutes past nine," exclaimed Mr Atheling, solemnly rising from the table. "I have not been so late for years—see what your nonsense has brought me to. Now, Mary, think it over reasonably, and I will hear all that you have to say to-night."

So Mr Atheling hastened to his desk to turn over this all-important matter as he walked and as he laboured. The Old Wood Lodge obliterated to the good man's vision the very folios of his daily companionship—old feelings, old incidents, old resentment and pugnacity, awoke again in his kindly but not altogether patient and self-commanded breast. The delight of being able to leave something—a certain patrimonial inheritance—to his son after him, gradually took possession of his mind and fancy; and the pleasant dignity of a house in the country—the happy power of sending off his wife and his children to the sweet air of his native place—won upon him gradually before he was aware. By slow degrees Mr Atheling brought himself to believe that it would be dishonourable to give up this relic of the family belongings, and make void the will of the dead. The Old Wood Lodge brightened before him into a very bower for his fair girls. The last poor remnant of his yeoman grandfather's little farm became a hereditary and romantic nucleus, which some other Atheling might yet make into a great estate. "There is Charlie—he will not always be a lawyer's clerk, that boy!" said his father to himself, with involuntary pride; and then he muttered under his breath, "and to give it up to *him*!"

Under this formidable conspiracy of emotions, the excellent Mr Atheling had no chance: old dislike, pungent and prevailing, though no one knew exactly its object or its cause, and present pride and tenderness still more strong and earnest, moved him beyond his power of resistance. There was no occasion for the attack, scientifically planned, which was to have been made upon him in the evening. If they had been meditating at home all day upon this delightful bit of romance in their own family history, and going over, with joy and enthusiasm, every room and closet in Miss Bridget's old house, Papa had been no less busy at the office. The uncertain tenor of a lawsuit had no longer any place in the good man's memory, and the equivocal advantage of the ruinous old house oppressed him no longer. He began to think, by an amiable and agreeable sophistry, self-delusive, that it was his sacred duty to carry out the wishes of the dead.

CHAPTER XXI
A LAW STUDENT

Steadily and laboriously these early summer days trudged on with Charlie, bringing no romantic visions nor dreams of brilliant fortune to tempt the imagination of the big boy. How his future looked to him no one knew. Charlie's aspirations—if he had any—dwelt private and secure within his own capacious breast. He was not dazzled by his sudden heirship of the Old Wood Lodge; he was not much disturbed by the growing fame of his sister; those sweet May mornings did not tempt him to the long ramble through the fields, which Agnes and Marian did their best to persuade him to. Charlie was not insensible to the exhilarating morning breeze, the greensward under foot, and the glory of those great thorn-hedges, white with the blossoms of the May—he was by no means a stoic either, as regarded his own ease and leisure, to which inferior considerations this stout youth attached their due importance; but still it remained absolute with Charlie, his own unfailing answer to all temptations—he had "something else to do!"

And his ordinary day's work was not of a very elevating character; he might have kept to that for years without acquiring much knowledge of his profession; and though he still was resolute to occupy no sham position, and determined that neither mother nor sisters should make sacrifices for him, Charlie felt no hesitation in making a brief and forcible statement to Mr Foggo on the subject. Mr Foggo listened with a pleased and gracious ear. "I'm not going to be a copying-clerk all my life," said Charlie. He was not much over seventeen; he was not remarkably well educated; he was a poor man's son, without connection, patronage, or influence. Notwithstanding, the acute old Scotsman looked at Charlie, lifting up the furrows of his brow, and pressing down his formidable upper-lip. The critical old lawyer smiled, but believed him. There was no possibility of questioning that obstinate big boy.

So Mr Foggo (acknowledged to be the most influential of chief clerks, and supposed to be a partner in the firm) made interest on behalf of Charlie, that he might have access, before business hours, to the law library of the house. The firm laughed, and gave permission graciously. The firm joked with its manager upon his credulity: a boy of seventeen coming at seven o'clock to voluntary study—and to take in a Scotsman—old Foggo! The firm grew perfectly jolly over this capital joke. Old Foggo smiled too, grimly, knowing better; and Charlie accordingly began his career.

It was not a very dazzling beginning. At seven o'clock the office was being dusted; in winter, at that hour, the fires were not alight, and extremely cross was the respectable matron who had charge of the same. Charlie stumbled over pails and brushes; dusters descended—unintentionally— upon his devoted head; he was pursued into every corner by his indefatigable enemy, and had to fly before her big broom with his big folio in his arms. But few people have pertinacity enough to maintain a perfectly unprofitable and fruitless warfare. Mrs Laundress, a humble prophetic symbol of that other virago, Fate, gave in to Charlie. He sat triumphant upon his high stool, no longer incommoded by dusters. While the moted sunbeams came dancing in through the dusty office window, throwing stray glances on his thick hair, and on the ponderous page before him, Charlie had a good round with his enemy, and got him down. The big boy plundered the big books with silent satisfaction, arranged his spoil on the secret shelves and pigeon- holes of that big brain of his, all ready and in trim for using; made his own comments on the whole complicated concern, and, with his whole mind bent on what was before him, mastered that, and thought of nothing else. Let nobody suppose he had the delight of a student in these strange and unattractive studies, or regarded with any degree of affectionateness the library of the House. Charlie looked at these volumes standing in dim rows, within their wired case, as Captain Bobadil might have looked at the army whom—one down and another come on—he meant to demolish, man by man. When he came to a knotty point, more hard than usual, the lad felt a stir of lively pleasure: he scorned a contemptible opponent, this stout young fighter, and gloried in a conquest which proved him, by stress and strain of all his healthful faculties, the better man. If they had been easy, Charlie would scarcely have cared for them. Certainly, mere literature, even were it as attractive as *Peter Simple*, could never have tempted him to the office at seven o'clock. Charlie stood by himself, like some primitive and original champion, secretly hammering out the armour which he was to wear in the field, and taking delight in the accomplishment of gyve and breastplate and morion, all proved and tested steel. Through the day he went about all his common businesses as sturdily and steadily as if his best ambition was to be a copying-clerk. If any one spoke of ambition, Charlie said "Stuff!" and no one ever heard a word of his own anticipations; but on he went, his foot ringing clear upon the pavement, his obstinate purpose holding as sure as if it were written on a rock. While all the household stirred and fluttered with the new tide of imaginative life which brightened upon it in all these gleams of the future, Charlie held stoutly on, pursuing his own straightforward and unattractive path. With his own kind of sympathy he eked out the pleasure of the family, and no one of them ever felt a lack in him; but nothing yet which had happened to the household in the slightest degree disturbed Charlie from his own bold, distinct, undemonstrative, and self-directed way.

CHAPTER XXII
ANOTHER EVENT

We will not attempt to describe the excitement, astonishment, and confusion produced in the house of the Athelings by the next communication received from Mr Burlington. It came at night, so that every one had the benefit, and its object was to announce the astounding and unexampled news of A Second Edition!

The letter dropped from Agnes's amazed fingers; Papa actually let fall his newspaper; and Charlie, disturbed at his grammar, rolled back the heavy waves of his brow, and laughed to himself. As for Mamma and Marian, each of them read the letter carefully over. There was no mistake about it—*Hope Hazelwood* was nearly out of print. True, Mr Burlington confessed that this first edition had been a small one, but the good taste of the public demanded a second; and the polite publisher begged to have an interview with Miss Atheling, to know whether she would choose to add or revise anything in the successful book.

Upon this there ensued a consultation. Mrs Atheling was doubtful as to the proprieties of the case; Papa was of opinion that the easiest and simplest plan was, that the girls should call; but Mamma, who was something of a timid nature, and withal a little punctilious, hesitated, and did not quite see which was best. Bellevue, doubtless, was very far out of the way, and the house, though so good a house, was not "like what Mr Burlington must have been accustomed to." The good mother was a long time making up her mind; but at last decided, with some perturbation, on the suggestion of Mr Atheling. "Yes, you can put on your muslin dresses; it is quite warm enough for them, and they always look well; and you must see, Marian, that your collars and sleeves are very nice, and your new bonnets. Yes, my dears, as there are two of you, I think you may call."

The morning came; and by this time it was the end of June, almost midsummer weather. Mrs Atheling herself, with the most anxious care, superintended the dressing of her daughters. They were dressed with the most perfect simplicity; and nobody could have supposed, to see the result, that any such elaborate overlooking had been bestowed upon their toilette. They were dressed well, in so far that their simple habiliments made no pretension above the plain pretty inexpensive reality. They were not intensely fashionable, like Mrs Tavistock's niece, who was a regular Islingtonian "swell" (if that most felicitous of epithets can be applied to anything feminine), and reminded everybody who saw her of work-rooms and dressmakers and plates of the fashions. Agnes and Marian, a hundred times plainer, were just so many times the better dressed. They were not quite skilled in the art of gloves—a difficult branch of costume, grievously embarrassing to those good girls, who had not much above a pair in three months, and were constrained to select thrifty colours; but otherwise Mrs Atheling herself was content with their appearance as they passed along Bellevue, brightening the sunny quiet road with their light figures and their bright eyes. They had a little awe upon them—that little shade of sweet embarrassment and expectation which gives one of its greatest charms to youth. They were talking over what they were to say, and marvelling how Mr Burlington would receive them; their young footsteps chiming as lightly as any music to her tender ear—their young voices sweeter than the singing of the birds, their bright looks more pleasant than the sunshine—it is not to be wondered at if the little street looked somewhat dim and shady to Mrs Atheling when these two young figures had passed out of it, and the mother stood alone at the window, looking at nothing better than the low brick-walls and closed doors of Laurel House and Green View.

And so they went away through the din and tumult of the great London, with their own bright young universe surrounding them, and their own sweet current of thought and emotion running as pure as if they had been passing through the sweetest fields of Arcadia. They had no eyes for impertinent gazers, if such things were in their way. Twenty stout footmen at their back could not have defended them so completely as did their own innocence and security. We confess they did not even shrink, with a proper sentimental horror, from all the din and all the commotion of this noonday Babylon; they liked their rapid glance at the wonderful shop-windows; they brightened more and more as their course lay along the gayest and most cheerful streets. It was pleasant to look at the maze of carriages, pleasant to see the throngs of people, exhilarating to be drawn along in this bright flood-tide and current of the world. But they grew a little nervous as they approached the house of Mr Burlington—a little more irregular in their pace, lingering and hastening as timidity or eagerness got the upper hand— and a great deal more silent, being fully occupied with anticipations of, and preparations for, this momentous interview. What should Agnes—what would Mr Burlington say?

This silence and shyness visibly increased as they came to the very scene and presence of the redoubtable publisher—where Agnes called the small attendant clerk in the outer office "Sir" and deferentially asked for Mr Burlington. When they had waited there for a few minutes, they were shown into a matted parlour containing a writing-table and a coal-scuttle, and three chairs. Mr Burlington would be disengaged in a few minutes, the little clerk informed them, as he solemnly displaced two of the chairs, an intimation that they were to sit down. They sat down accordingly, with the most matter-of-course obedience, and held their breath as they listened for the coming steps of Mr Burlington. But the minutes passed, and Mr Burlington did not come. They began to look round with extreme interest and curiosity, augmented all the more by their awe. There was nothing in the least interesting in this bare little apartment, but their young imaginations could make a great deal out of nothing. At Mr Burlington's door stood a carriage, with a grand powdered coachman on the box, and the most superb of flunkies gracefully lounging before the door. No doubt Mr Burlington was engaged with the owner of all this splendour. Immediately they ran over all the great names they could remember, forgetting for the moment that authors, even of the greatest, are not much given, as a general principle, to gilded coaches and flunkies of renown. Who could it be?

When they were in the very height of their guessing, the door suddenly opened. They both rose with a start; but it was only the clerk, who asked them to follow him to the presence of Mr Burlington. They went noiselessly along the long matted passage after their conductor, who was not much of a Ganymede. At the very end, a door stood open, and there were two figures half visible between them and a big round-headed window, full of somewhat pale and cloudy sky. These two people turned round, as some faint sound of the footsteps of Ganymede struck aside from the matting. "Oh, what a lovely creature!—what a beautiful girl! Now I do hope that is the one!" cried, most audibly, a feminine voice. Marian, knowing by instinct that she was meant, shrank back grievously discomfited. Even Agnes was somewhat dismayed by such a preface to their interview; but Ganymede was a trained creature, and much above the weakness of a smile or hesitation—*he* pressed on unmoved, and hurried them into the presence and the sanctum of Mr Burlington. They came into the full light of the big window, shy, timid, and graceful, having very little self-possession to boast of, their hearts beating, their colour rising—and for the moment it was scarcely possible to distinguish which was the beautiful sister; for Agnes was very near as pretty as Marian in the glow and agitation of her heart.

CHAPTER XXIII
A NEW FRIEND

The big window very nearly filled up the whole room. The little place had once been the inmost heart of a long suite of apartments when this was a fashionable house—now it was an odd little nook of seclusion, with panelled walls, painted of so light a colour as to look almost white in the great overflow of daylight; and what had looked like a pale array of clouds in the window at a little distance, made itself out now to be various blocks and projections of white-washed wall pressing very close on every side, and leaving only in the upper half-circle a clear bit of real clouds and unmistakable sky. The room had a little table, a very few chairs, and the minutest and most antique of Turkey carpets laid over the matting. The walls were very high; there was not even a familiar coal-scuttle to lessen the solemnity of the publisher's retreat and sanctuary; and Mr Burlington was not alone.

And even the inexperienced eyes of Agnes and Marian were not slow to understand that the lady who stood by Mr Burlington's little table was a genuine fine lady, one of that marvellous and unknown species which flourishes in novels, but never had been visible in such a humble hemisphere as the world of Bellevue. She was young still, but had been younger, and she remained rich in that sweetest of all mere external beauties, the splendid English complexion, that lovely bloom and fairness, which is by no means confined to the flush of youth. She looked beautiful by favour of these natural roses and lilies, but she was not beautiful in reality from any other cause. She was lively, good-natured, and exuberant to an extent which amazed these shy young creatures, brought up under the quiet shadow of propriety, and accustomed to the genteel deportment of Bellevue. They, in their simple girlish dress, in their blushes, diffidence, and hesitation—and she, accustomed to see everything yielding to her pretty caprices, arbitrary, coquettish, irresistible, half a spoiled child and half a woman of the world—they stood together, in the broad white light of that big window, like people born in different planets. They could scarcely form the slightest conception of each other. Nature itself had made difference enough; but how is it possible to estimate the astonishing difference between Mayfair and Bellevue?

"Pray introduce me, Mr Burlington; oh pray introduce me!" cried this pretty vision before Mr Burlington himself had done more than bow to his shy young visitors. "I am delighted to know the author of *Hope Hazlewood*! charmed to be acquainted with Miss Atheling! My dear child, how is it possible, at your age, to know so much of the world?"

"It is my sister," said Marian very shyly, almost under her breath. Marian was much disturbed by this mistake of identity; it had never occurred to her before that any one could possibly be at a loss for the real Miss Atheling. The younger sister was somewhat indignant at so strange a mistake.

"Now that is right! that is poetic justice! that is a proper distribution of gifts!" said the lady, clasping her hands with a pretty gesture of approval. "If you will not introduce me, I shall be compelled to do it myself, Mr Burlington: Mrs Edgerley. I am charmed to be the first to make your acquaintance; we were all dying to know the author of *Hope Hazlewood*. What a charming book it is! I say there has been nothing like it since *Ellen Fullarton*, and dear Theodosia herself entirely agrees with me. You are staying in town? Oh I am delighted! You must let me see a great deal of you, you must indeed; and I shall be charmed to introduce you to Lady Theodosia, whose sweet books every one loves. Pray, Mr Burlington, have you any very great secrets to say to these young ladies, for I want so much to persuade them to come with me?"

"I shall not detain Miss Atheling," said the publisher, with a bow, and the ghost of a smile: "we will bring out the second edition in a week or two; a very pleasant task, I assure you, and one which repays us for our anxiety. Now, how about a preface? I shall be delighted to attend to your wishes."

But Agnes, who had thought so much about him beforehand, had been too much occupied hitherto to do more than glance at Mr Burlington. She scarcely looked up now, when every one was looking at her, but said, very low and with embarrassment, that she did not think she had any wishes—that she left it entirely to Mr Burlington—he must know best.

"Then we shall have no preface?" said Mr Burlington, deferentially.

"No," said Agnes, faltering a little, and glancing up to see if he approved; "for indeed I do not think I have anything to say."

"Oh that is what a preface is made for," cried the pretty Mrs Edgerley. "You dear innocent child, do you never speak except when you have something to say? Delightful! charming! I shall not venture to introduce you to Lady Theodosia; if she but knew, how she would envy me! You must come home with me to luncheon—you positively must; for I am quite sure Mr Burlington has not another word to say."

The two girls drew back a little, and exchanged glances. "Indeed you are very good, but we must go home," said Agnes, not very well aware what she was saying.

"No, you must come with me—you must positively; I should break my heart," said their new acquaintance, with a pretty affectation of caprice and despotism altogether new to the astonished girls. "Oh, I assure you no one resists me. Your mamma will not have a word to say if you tell her it is Mrs Edgerley. Good morning, Mr Burlington; how fortunate I was to call to-day!"

So saying, this lady of magic swept out, rustling through the long matted passages, and carrying her captives, half delighted, half afraid, in her train. They were too shy by far to make a pause and a commotion by resisting; they had nothing of the self-possession of the trained young ladies of society. The natural impulse of doing what they were told was very strong upon them, and before they were half aware, or had time to consider, they were shut into the carriage by the sublime flunky, and drove off into those dazzling and undiscovered regions, as strange to them as Lapland or Siberia, where dwells The World. Agnes was placed by the side of the enchantress; Marian sat shyly opposite, rather more afraid of Mrs Edgerley's admiring glance than she had ever been before of the gaze of strangers. It seemed like witchcraft and sudden magic—half-an-hour ago sitting in the little waiting-room, looking out upon the fairy chariot, and now rolling along in its perfumy and warm enclosure over the aristocratic stones of St James's. The girls were bewildered with their marvellous position, and could not make it out, while into their perplexity stole an occasional thought of what Mamma would say, and how very anxious she would grow if they did not get soon home.

Mrs Edgerley in the meanwhile ran on with a flutter of talk and enthusiasm, pretty gestures, and rapid inquiries, so close and constant that there was little room for answer and none for comment. And then, long before they could be at their ease in the carriage, it drew up, making a magnificent commotion, before a door which opened immediately to admit the mistress of the house. Agnes and Marian followed her humbly as she hastened up-stairs. They were bewildered with the long suite of lofty apartments through which their conductress hurried, scarcely aware, they supposed, that they, not knowing what else to do, followed where she led, till they came at last to a pretty boudoir, furnished, as they both described it unanimously, "like the Arabian Nights!" Here Mrs Edgerley found some letters, the object, as it seemed, of her search, and good-naturedly paused, with her correspondence in her hand, to point out to them the Park, which could be seen from the window, and the books upon the tables. Then she left them, looking at each other doubtfully, and half afraid to remain. "Oh, Agnes, what will mamma say?" whispered Marian. All their innocent lives, until this day, they had never made a visit to any one without the permission or sanction of Mamma.

"We could not help it," said Agnes. That was very true; so with a relieved conscience, but very shyly, they turned over the pretty picture-books, the pretty nicknacks, all the elegant nothings of Mrs Edgerley's pretty bower. Good Mrs Atheling could very seldom be tempted to buy anything that was not useful, and there was scarcely a single article in the whole house at home which was not good for something. This being the case, it is easy to conceive with what perverse youthful delight the girls contemplated the hosts of pretty things around, which were of no use whatever, nor good for anything in the world. It gave them an idea of exuberance, of magnificence, of prodigality, more than the substantial magnitude of the great house or the handsome equipage. Besides, they were alone for the moment, and so much less embarrassed, and the rose-coloured atmosphere charmed them all the more that they were quite unaccustomed to it. Yet they spoke to each other in whispers as they peeped into the sunny Park, all bright and green in the sunshine, and marvelled much what Mamma would say, and how they should get home.

When Mrs Edgerley returned to them, they were stooping over the table together, looking over some of the most splendid of the "illustrated editions" of this age of sumptuous bookmaking. When they saw their patroness they started, and drew a little apart from each other. She came towards them through the great drawing-room, radiant and rustling, and they looked at her with shy admiration. They were by no means sure of their own position, but their new acquaintance certainly was the kindest and most delightful of all sudden friends.

"Do you forgive me for leaving you?" said Mrs Edgerley, holding out both her pretty hands; "but now we must not wait here any longer, but go to luncheon, where we shall be all by ourselves, quite a snug little party; and now, you dear child, come and tell me everything about it. What was it that first made you think of writing that charming book?"

Mrs Edgerley had drawn Agnes's arm within her own, a little to the discomposure of the shy young genius, and, followed closely by Marian, led them down stairs. Agnes made no answer in her confusion. Then they came to a pretty apartment on the lower floor, with a broad window looking out to the Park. The table was near the window; the pretty scene outside belonged to the little group within, as they placed themselves at the table, and the room itself was green and cool and pleasant, not at all splendid, lined with books, and luxurious with easy-chairs. There was a simple vase upon the table, full of roses, but there was no profusion of prettinesses here.

"This is my own study; I bring every one to see it. Is it not a charming little room?" said Mrs Edgerley (it would have contained both the parlours and the two best bedrooms of Number Ten, Bellevue); "but now I am quite dying to hear—really, how did it come into your head to write that delightful book?"

"Indeed I do not know," said Agnes, smiling and blushing. It seemed perfectly natural that the book should have made so mighty a sensation, and yet it was rather embarrassing, after all.

"I think because she could not help it," said Marian shyly, her beautiful face lighting up as she spoke with a sweet suffusion of colour. Their hearts were beginning to open to the kindness of their new friend.

"And you are so pleased and so proud of your sister—I am sure you are—it is positively delightful," said Mrs Edgerley. "Now tell me, were you not quite heartbroken when you finished it—such a delightful interest one feels in one's characters—such an object it is to live for, is it not? The first week after my first work was finished I was *triste* beyond description. I am sure you must have been quite miserable when you were obliged to come to an end."

The sisters glanced at each other rather doubtfully across the table. Everybody else seemed to have feelings so much more elevated than they— for they both remembered with a pang of shame that Agnes had actually been glad and jubilant when this first great work was done.

"And such a sweet heroine—such a charming character!" said Mrs Edgerley. "Ah, I perceive you have taken your sister for your model, and now I shall always feel sure that she is Hope Hazlewood; but at your age I cannot conceive where you got so much knowledge of the world. Do you go out a great deal? do you see a great many people? But indeed, to tell the truth," said Mrs Edgerley, with a pretty laugh, "I do believe you have no right to see any one yet. You ought to be in the schoolroom, young creatures like you. Are you both *out*?"

This was an extremely puzzling question, and some answer was necessary this time. The girls again looked at each other, blushing over neck and brow. In their simple honesty they thought themselves bound to make a statement of their true condition—what Miss Willsie would have called "their rank in life."

"We see very few people. In our circumstances people do not speak about coming out," said Agnes, hesitating and doubtful—the young author had no great gift of elegant expression. But in fact Mrs Edgerley did not care in the slightest degree about their "circumstances." She was a hundred times more indifferent on that subject than any genteel and respectable matron in all Bellevue.

"Oh then, that is so much better," said Mrs Edgerley, "for I see you must have been observing character all your life. It is, after all, the most delightful study; but such an eye for individuality! and so young! I declare I shall be quite afraid to make friends with you."

"Indeed, I do not know at all about character," said Agnes hurriedly, as with her pretty little ringing laugh, Mrs Edgerley broke off in a pretty affected trepidation; but their patroness shook her hand at her, and turned away in a graceful little terror.

"I am sure she must be the most dreadful critic, and keep you quite in awe of her," said their new friend, turning to Marian. "But now pray tell me your names. I have such an interest in knowing every one's Christian name; there is so much character in them. I do think that is the real advantage of a title. There is dear Lady Theodosia, for instance: suppose her family had been commoners, and she had been called Miss Piper! Frightful! odious! almost enough to make one do some harm to oneself, or get married. And now tell me what are your names?"

"My sister is Agnes, and I am Marian," said the younger. Now we are obliged to confess that by this time, though Mrs Edgerley answered with the sweetest and most affectionate of smiles and a glance of real admiration, she began to feel the novelty wear off, and flagged a little in her sudden enthusiasm. It was clear to her young visitors that she did not at all attend to the answer, despite the interest with which she had asked the question. A shade of weariness, half involuntary, half of will and purpose, came over her face. She rushed away immediately upon another subject; asked another question with great concern, and was completely indifferent to the answer. The girls were not used to this phenomenon, and did not understand it; but at last, after hesitating and doubting, and consulting each other by glances, Agnes made a shy movement of departure, and said Mamma would be anxious, and they should have to go away.

"The carriage is at the door, I believe," said Mrs Edgerley, with her sweet smile; "for of course you must let me send you home—positively you must, my love. You are a great author, but you are a young lady, and your sister is much too pretty to walk about alone. Delighted to have seen you both! Oh, I shall write to you very soon; do not fear. Everybody wants to make your acquaintance. I shall be besieged for introductions. You are engaged to me for Thursday next week, remember! I never forgive any one who disappoints me. Good-by! Adieu! I am charmed to have met you both."

While this valedictory address was being said, the girls were slowly making progress to the door; then they were ushered out solemnly to the carriage which waited for them. They obeyed their fate in their going as they did in their coming. They could not help themselves; and with mingled fright, agitation, and pleasure, were once more shut up by that superbest of flunkies, but drove off at a slow pace, retarded by the intense bewilderment of the magnificent coachman as to the locality of Bellevue.

CHAPTER XXIV
GOING HOME

Driving slowly along while the coachman ruminated, Agnes and Marian, in awe and astonishment, looked in each other's faces—then they put up their hands simultaneously to their faces, which were a little heated with the extreme confusion, embarrassment, and wonder of the last two hours— lastly, they both fell into a little outburst of low and somewhat tremulous laughter—laughing in a whisper, if that is possible—and laughing, not because they were very merry, but because, in their extreme amazement, no other expression of their sentiments occurred to them. Were they two enchanted princesses? and had they been in fairyland?

"Oh Agnes!" exclaimed Marian under her breath, "what will mamma say?"

"I do not think mamma can be angry," said Agnes, who had gained some courage, "for I am sure we could not help ourselves. What could we do?—but when they see us coming home like this—oh May!"

There was another pause. "I wonder very much what she has written. We have never heard of her," said Marian, "and yet I suppose she must be quite a great author. How respectful Mr Burlington was! I am afraid it will not be good for you, Agnes, that we live so much out of the world—you ought to know people's names at least."

Agnes did not dispute this advantage. "But I don't quite think she can be a great author," said the young genius, looking somewhat puzzled, "though I am sure she was very kind—how kind she was, Marian! And do you think she really wants us to go on Thursday? Oh, I wonder what mamma will say!"

As this was the burden of the whole conversation, constantly recurring, as every new phase of the question was discussed, the conversation itself was not quite adapted for formal record. While it proceeded, the magnificent coachman blundered towards the unknown regions of Islington, much marvelling, in his lofty and elevated intelligence, what sort of people his mistress's new acquaintances could be. They reached Bellevue at last by a grievous roundabout. What a sound and commotion they made in this quiet place, where a doctor's brougham was the most fashionable of equipages, and a pair of horses an unknown glory! The dash of that magnificent drawing-up startled the whole neighbourhood, and the population of Laurel House and Buena Vista flew to their bedroom windows when the big footman made that prodigious assault upon the knocker of Number Ten. Then came the noise of letting down the steps and opening the carriage door; then the girls alighted, almost as timid as Susan, who stood scared and terror-stricken within the door; and then Agnes, in sudden temerity, but with a degree of respectfulness, offered, to the acceptance of the footman, a precious golden half-sovereign, intrusted to her by her mother this morning, in case they should want anything. Poor Mrs Atheling, sitting petrified in her husband's easy-chair, did not know how the coin was being disposed of. They came in—the humble door was closed—they stood again in the close little hall, with its pegs and its painted oil-cloth—what a difference!—while the fairy coach and the magical bay-horses, the solemn coachman and the superb flunky, drove back into the world again with a splendid commotion, which deafened the ears and fluttered the heart of all Bellevue.

"My dears, where have you been? What have you been doing, girls? Was that Mr Burlington's carriage? Have you seen any one? Where have you been?" asked Mrs Atheling, while Agnes cried eagerly, "Mamma, you are not to be angry!" and Marian answered, "Oh, mamma! we have been in fairyland!"

And then they sat down upon the old hair-cloth sofa beside the family table, upon which, its sole ornaments, stood Mrs Atheling's full work-basket, and some old toys of Bell's and Beau's; and thus, sometimes speaking together, sometimes interrupting each other, with numberless corrections on the part of Marian and supplementary remarks from Agnes, they told their astonishing story. They had leisure now to enjoy all they had seen and heard when they were safe in their own house, and reporting it all to Mamma. They described everything, remembered everything, went over every word and gesture of Mrs Edgerley, from her first appearance in Mr Burlington's room until their parting with her; and Marian faithfully recorded all her compliments to *Hope Hazlewood*, and Agnes her admiration of Marian. It was the prettiest scene in the world to see them both, flushed and animated, breaking in, each upon the other's narrative, contradicting each other, after a fashion; remonstrating "Oh Agnes!" explaining, and adding description to description; while the mother sat before them in her easy-chair, sometimes quietly wiping her eyes, sometimes interfering or commanding, "One at a time, my dears," and all the time thinking to herself that the honours that were paid to "girls like these!" were no such wonder after all. And indeed Mrs Atheling would not be sufficiently amazed at all this grand and wonderful story. She was extremely touched and affected by the kindness of Mrs Edgerley, and dazzled with the prospect of all the great people who were waiting with so much anxiety to make acquaintance with the author of *Hope Hazlewood*, but she was by no means properly *surprised*.

"My dears, I foresaw how it would be," said Mrs Atheling with her simple wisdom. "I knew quite well all this must happen, Agnes. I have not read about famous people for nothing, though I never said much about it. To be sure, my dear, I knew people would appreciate you—it is quite natural—it is quite proper, my dear child! I know they will never make you forget what is right, and your duty, let them flatter as they will!"

Mrs Atheling said this with a little effusion, and with wet eyes. Agnes hung her head, blushed very deeply, grew extremely grave for a moment, but concluded by glancing up suddenly again with a little overflow of laughter. In the midst of all, she could not help recollecting how perfectly ridiculous it was to make all this commotion about *her*. "Me!" said Agnes with a start; "they will find me out directly—they must, mamma. You know I cannot talk or do anything; and indeed everybody that knew me would laugh to think of people seeing anything in *me*!"

Now this was perfectly true, though the mother and the sister, for the moment, were not quite inclined to sanction it. Agnes was neither brilliant nor remarkable, though she had genius, and was, at twenty and a half, a successful author in her way. As she woke from her first awe and amazement, Agnes began to find out the ludicrous side of her new fame. It was all very well to like the book; there was some reason in that, the young author admitted candidly; but surely those people must expect something very different from the reality, who were about to besiege Mrs Edgerley for introductions to "*me*!"

However, it was very easy to forget this part of the subject in returning to the dawn of social patronage, and in anticipating the invitation they had received. Mrs Atheling, too, was somewhat disappointed that they had made so little acquaintance with Mr Burlington, and could scarcely even describe him, how he looked or what he said. Mr Burlington had quite gone down in the estimation of the girls. His lady client had entirely eclipsed, overshadowed, and taken the glory out of the publisher. The talk was all of Mrs Edgerley, her beauty, her kindness, her great house, her approaching party. They began already to be agitated about this, remembering with terror the important article of dress, and the simple nature and small variety of their united wardrobe. Before they had been an hour at home, Miss Willsie made an abrupt and sudden visit from Killiecrankie Lodge, to ascertain all about the extraordinary apparition of the carriage, and to find out where the girls had been; and it did not lessen their own excitement to discover the extent of the commotion which they had caused in Bellevue. The only drawback was, that a second telling of the story was not practicable for the instruction and advantage of Papa—for, for the first time in a dozen years, Mr Atheling, all by himself, and solitary, was away from home.

CHAPTER XXV
PAPA'S OPINION

Papa was away from home. That very day on which the charmed light of society first shone upon his girls, Papa, acting under the instructions of a family conference, hurried at railway speed to the important neighbourhood of the Old Wood Lodge. He was to be gone three days, and during that time his household constituents expected an entire settlement of the doubtful and difficult question which concerned their inheritance. Charlie, perhaps, might have some hesitation on the subject, but all the rest of the family believed devoutly in the infallible wisdom and prowess of Papa.

Yet it was rather disappointing that he should be absent at such a crisis as this, when there was so much to tell him. They had to wonder every day what he would think of the adventure of Agnes and Marian, and how contemplate their entrance into the world; and great was the family satisfaction at the day and hour of his return. Fortunately it was evening; the family tea-table was spread with unusual care, and the best china shone and glistened in the sunshine, as Agnes, Marian, and Charlie set out for the railway to meet their father. They went along together very happily, excited by the expectation of all there was to tell, and all there was to hear. The suburban roads were full of leisurely people, gossiping, or meditating like old Isaac at eventide, with a breath of the fields before them, and the big boom of the great city filling all the air behind. The sun slanted over the homely but pleasant scene, making a glorious tissue of the rising smoke, and brightening the dusky branches of the wayside trees. "If we could but live in the country!" said Agnes, pausing, and turning round to trace the long sun-bright line of road, falling off into that imaginary Arcadia, or rather into the horizon, with its verge of sunny and dewy fields. The dew falls upon the daisies even in the vicinity of Islington—let students of natural history bear this significant fact in mind.

"Stuff! the train's in," said Charlie, dragging along his half-reluctant sister, who, quite proud of his bigness and manly stature, had taken his arm. "Charlie, don't make such strides—who do you think can keep up with you?" said Marian. Charlie laughed with the natural triumphant malice of a younger brother; he was perfectly indifferent to the fact that one of them was a genius and the other a beauty; but he liked to claim a certain manly and protective superiority over "the girls."

To the great triumph, however, of these victims of Charlie's obstinate will, the train was not in, and they had to walk about upon the platform for full five minutes, pulling (figuratively) his big red ear, and waiting for the exemplary second-class passenger, who was scrupulous to travel by that golden mean of respectability, and would on no account have put up with a parliamentary train. Happy Papa, it was better than Mrs Edgerley's magnificent pair of bays pawing in superb impatience the plebeian causeway. He caught a glimpse of three eager faces as he looked out of his little window—two pretty figures springing forward, one big one holding back, and remonstrating. "Why, you'll lose him in the crowd—do you hear?" cried Charlie. "What good could you do, a parcel of girls? See! you stand here, and I'll fetch my father out."

Grievously against their will, the girls obeyed. Papa was safely evolved out of the crowd, and went off at once between his daughters, leaving Charlie to follow—which Charlie did accordingly, with Mr Atheling's greatcoat in one hand and travelling-bag in the other. They made quite a little procession as they went home, Marian half dancing as she clasped Papa's arm, and tantalised him with hints of their wondrous tale; Agnes walking very demurely on the other side, with a pretence of rebuking her giddy sister; Charlie trudging with his burden in the rear. By way of assuring him that he was not to know till they got home, Papa was put in possession of all the main facts of their adventure, before they came near enough to see two small faces at the bright open window, shouting with impatience to see him. Happy Papa! it was almost worth being away a year, instead of three days, to get such a welcome home.

"Well, but who is this fine lady—and how were you introduced to her— and what's all this about a carriage?" said Papa. "Here's Bell and Beau, with all their good sense, reduced to be as crazy as the rest of you. What's this about a carriage?"

For Bell and Beau, we are constrained to confess, had made immense ado about the "two geegees" ever since these fabulous and extraordinary animals drew up before the gate with that magnificent din and concussion which shook to its inmost heart the quiet of Bellevue.

"Oh, it is Mrs Edgerley's, papa," said Marian; "such a beautiful pair of bay horses—she sent us home in it—and we met her at Mr Burlington's, and we went to luncheon at her house—and we are going there again on Thursday to a great party. She says everybody wishes to see Agnes; she thinks there never was a book like *Hope*. She is very pretty, and has the grandest house, and is kinder than anybody I ever saw. You never saw such splendid horses. Oh, mamma, how pleasant it would be to keep a carriage! I wonder if Agnes will ever be as rich as Mrs Edgerley; but then, though *she* is an author, she is a great lady besides."

"Edgerley!" said Mr Atheling; "do you know, I heard that name at the Old Wood Lodge."

"But, papa, what about the Lodge? you have never told us yet: is it as pretty as you thought it was? Can we go to live there? Is there a garden? I am sure *now*," said Agnes, blushing with pleasure, "that we will have money enough to go down there—all of us—mamma, and Bell and Beau!"

"I don't deny it's rather a pretty place," said Mr Atheling; "and I thought of Agnes immediately when I looked out from the windows. There is a view for you! Do you remember it, Mary?—the town below, and the wood behind, and the river winding about everywhere. Well, I confess to you it *is* pretty, and not in such bad order either, considering all things; and nothing said against our title yet, Mr Lewis tells me. Do you know, children, if you were really to go down and take possession, and then my lord made any attempt against us, I should be tempted to stand out against him, cost what it might?"

"Then, papa, we ought to go immediately," said Marian. "To be sure, you should stand out—it belonged to our family; what has anybody else got to do with it? And I tell you, Charlie, you ought to read up all about it, and make quite sure, and let the gentleman know the real law."

"Stuff! I'll mind my own business," said Charlie. Charlie did not choose to have any allusion made to his private studies.

"And there are several people there who remember us, Mary," said Mr Atheling. "My lord is not at home—that is one good thing; but I met a youth at Winterbourne yesterday, who lives at the Hall they say, and is a—a—sort of a son; a fine boy, with a haughty look, more like the old lord a great deal. And what did you say about Edgerley? There's one of the Rivers's married to an Edgerley. I won't have such an acquaintance, if it turns out one of them."

"Why, William?" said Mrs Atheling. "Fathers and daughters are seldom very much like each other. I do not care much about such an acquaintance myself," added the good mother, in a moralising tone. "For though it may be very pleasant for the girls at first, I do not think it is good, as Miss Willsie says, to have friends far out of our own rank of life. My dear, Miss Willsie is very sensible, though she is not always pleasant; and I am sure you never can be very easy or comfortable with people whom you cannot have at your own house; and you know such a great lady as that could not come *here*."

Agnes and Marian cast simultaneous glances round the room—it was impossible to deny that Mrs Atheling was right.

"But then the Old Wood Lodge, mamma!" cried Agnes, with sudden relief and enthusiasm. "There we could receive any one—anybody could come to see us in the country. If the furniture is not very good, we can improve it a little. For you know, mamma——." Agnes once more blushed with shy delight and satisfaction, but came to a sudden conclusion there, and said no more.

"Yes, my dear, I know," said Mrs Atheling, with a slight sigh, and a careful financial brow; "but when your fortune comes, papa must lay it by for you, Agnes, or invest it. William, what did you say it would be best to do?"

Mr Atheling immediately entered *con amore* into a consideration of the best means of disposing of this fabulous and unarrived fortune. But the girls looked blank when they heard of interest and percentage; they did not appreciate the benefits of laying by.

"Are we to have no good of it, then, at all?" said Agnes disconsolately.

Mr Atheling's kind heart could not resist an appeal like this. "Yes, Mary, they must have their pleasure," said Papa; "it will not matter much to Agnes's fortune, the little sum that they will spend on the journey, or the new house. No, you must go by all means; I shall fancy it is in mourning for poor old Aunt Bridget, till my girls are there to pull her roses. If I knew you were all there, I should begin to think again that Winterbourne and Badgely Wood were the sweetest places in the world."

"And there any one could come to see us," said Marian, clapping her hands. "Oh, papa, what a good thing for Agnes that Aunt Bridget left you the Old Wood Lodge!"

CHAPTER XXVI
MRS EDGERLY'S THURSDAY

Mr Atheling's visit to the country had, after all, not been so necessary as the family supposed; no one seemed disposed to pounce upon the small bequest of Miss Bridget. The Hall took no notice either of the death or the will which changed the proprietorship of the Old Wood Lodge. It remained intact and unvisited, dilapidated and picturesque, with Miss Bridget's old furniture in its familiar place, and her old maid in possession. The roses began to brush the little parlour window, and thrust their young buds against the panes, from which no one now looked out upon their sweetness. Papa himself, though his heart beat high to think of his own beautiful children blooming in this retired and pleasant place, wept a kindly tear for his old aunt, as he stood in the chamber of her long occupation, and found how empty and mournful was this well-known room. It was a quaint and touching mausoleum, full of relics; and good Mr Atheling felt himself more and more bound to carry out the old lady's wishes as he stood in the vacant room.

And then it would be such a good thing for Agnes! That was the most flattering and pleasant view of the subject possible; and ambitious ideas of making the Old Wood Lodge the prettiest of country cottages, entered the imagination of the house. It was pretty enough for anything, Papa said, looking as he spoke at his beautiful Marian, who was precisely in the same condition; and if some undefined notion of a prince of romance, carrying off from the old cottage the sweetest bride in the world, did flash across the thoughts of the father and mother, who would be hard enough to blame so natural a vision? As for Marian herself, she thought of nothing but Agnes, unless, indeed, it was Mrs Edgerley's party; and there must, indeed, have been quite a moral earthquake in London had all the invitees to this same party been as much disturbed about it as these two sisters. They wondered a hundred times in a day if it was quite right to go without any further invitation—if Mrs Edgerley would write to them—who would be there? and finally, and most momentous of all, if it would be quite proper to go in those simple white dresses, which were, in fact, the only dresses they could wear. Over these girlish robes there was great discussion, and councils manifold; people, however, who have positively no choice, have facilities for making up their minds unknown to more encumbered individuals, and certainly there was no alternative here.

Another of these much discussed questions was likewise very shortly set to rest. Mrs Edgerley did write to Agnes the most affectionate and emphatic of notes—deeply, doubly underscored in every fourth word, adjuring her to "*remember* that I NEVER *forgive* any one who *forgets* my *Thursday*." Nobody could possibly be more innocent of this unpardonable crime than Agnes and Marian, from whose innocent minds, since they first heard of it, Mrs Edgerley's Thursday had scarcely been absent for an hour at a stretch; but they were mightily gratified with this reminder, and excited beyond measure with the prospect before them. They had also ascertained with much care and research the names of their new acquaintance's works—of which one was called *Fashion,* one *Coquetry,* and one *The Beau Monde.* On the title-page of these famous productions she was called the Honourable Mrs Edgerley—a distinction not known to them before; and the girls read with devotion the three sets of three volumes each, by which their distinguished friend had made herself immortal. These books were not at all like *Hope Hazlewood.* It was not indeed very easy to define what they were like; they were very fine, full of splendid upholstery and elevated sentiments, diamonds of the finest water, and passions of the loftiest strain. The girls prudently reserved their judgment on the matter. "It is only some people who can write good books," said Marian, in the tone of an indulgent critic; and nobody disputed the self-evident truth.

Meanwhile Mr Foggo continued to pay his usual visit every night, and Miss Willsie, somewhat curious and full of disapprovals, "looked in" through the day. Miss Willsie, who in secret knew *Hope Hazlewood* nearly by heart, disapproved of everything. If there was one thing she did not like, it was young people setting up their opinion, and especially writing books; and if there was one thing she could not bear, it was to see folk in a middling way of life aiming to be like their betters. Miss Willsie "could not put up with" Mrs Edgerley's presumption in sending the girls home in her carriage; she thought it was just as much as taunting decent folk because they had no carriage of their own. Altogether the mistress of Killiecrankie was out of temper, and would not be pleased—nothing satisfied her; and she groaned in spirit over the vanity of her young *protégés*.

"Silly things!" said Miss Willsie, as she came in on the eventful morning of Thursday itself, that golden day; "do you really think there's satisfaction in such vanities? Do you think any person finds happiness in the pleasures of this world?"

"Oh, Miss Willsie! if they were not very pleasant, why should people be so frightened for them?" cried Marian, who was carefully trimming, with some of her mother's lace, the aforesaid white dress.

"And then we are not trying to *find* happiness," said Agnes, looking up from her similar occupation with a radiant face, and a momentary perception of the philosophy of the matter. After all, that made a wonderful difference. Miss Willsie was far too Scotch to remain unimpressed by the logical distinction.

"Well, that's true," acknowledged Miss Willsie; "but you're no to think I approve of such a way of spending your happiness, though ye have got it, ye young prodigals. If there is one thing I cannot endure, it's countenancing the like of you in your nonsense and extravagance; but I'm no for doing things by halves either—Here!"

Saying which, Miss Willsie laid a parcel upon the table and disappeared instantly, opening the door for herself, and closing it after her with the briskest energy. There was not much time lost in examining the parcel; and within it, in a double wrapper, lay two little pairs of satin shoes, the whitest, daintiest, prettiest in the world.

Cinderella's glass slippers! But Cinderella in the story was not half so much disturbed as these two girls. It seemed just the last proof wanting of the interest all the world took in this momentous and eventful evening. Miss Willsie, the general critic and censor, who approved of nothing! If it had not been for a little proper pride in the presence of Susan, who just then entered the parlour, Marian and Agnes would have been disposed for half a minute to celebrate this pleasure, in true feminine fashion, by a very little "cry."

And then came the momentous duties of the toilette. The little white bedchamber looked whiter to-night than it had done all its days before, under the combined lustre of the white dresses, the white ribbons, and the white shoes. They were both so young and both so bright that their colourless and simple costume looked in the prettiest harmony imaginable with their sweet youth—which was all the more fortunate, that they could not help themselves, and had nothing else to choose. One of those useful and nondescript vehicles called "flies" stood at the door. Charlie, with his hat on, half laughing, half ashamed of his office, lingered in the hall, waiting to accompany them. They kissed Bell and Beau (dreadfully late for this one night, and in the highest state of exultation) with solemnity—submitted themselves to a last inspection on the part of Mrs Atheling, and with a little fright and sudden terror were put into the "carriage." Then the carriage drove away through the late summer twilight, rambling into the distance and the darkness. Then at last Mamma ventured to drop into the easy-chair, and rest for a moment from her labours and her anxieties. At this great crisis of the family history, small events looked great events to Mrs Atheling; as if they had been going out upon a momentous enterprise, this good mother paused awhile in the darkness, and blessed them in her heart.

CHAPTER XXVII
THE WORLD

They were bewildered, yet they lost nothing of the scene. The great rooms radiant with light, misty with hangings, gleaming with mirrors—the magnificent staircase up which they passed, they never could tell how, ashamed of the echo of their own names—the beautiful enchantress of a hostess, who bestowed upon each of them that light perfumy kiss of welcome, at the momentary touch of which the girls blushed and trembled—the strange faces everywhere around them—their own confusion, and the shyness which they thought so awkward. Though all these things together united to form a dazzling jumble for the first moment, the incoherence of the vision lasted no longer. With a touch of kindness Mrs Edgerley led them (for of course they were scrupulously early, and punctual to the hour) to her pretty boudoir, where they had been before, and which was not so bright nor like to be so thronged as the larger rooms. Here already a young matron sat in state, with a little circle of worshippers. Mrs Edgerley broke into the midst of them to introduce to the throned lady her young strangers. "They have no one with them—pray let them be beside you," whispered the beautiful hostess to her beautiful guest. The lady bowed, and stared, and assented. When Mrs Edgerley left them, Agnes and Marian looked after her wistfully, the only face they had ever seen before, and stood together in their shy irresolute grace, blushing, discouraged, and afraid. They supposed it was not right to speak to any one whom they had not been introduced to; but no one gave them any inconvenience for the moment in the matter of conversation. They stood for a short time shyly, expecting some notice from their newly-elected chaperone, but she had half-a-dozen flirtations in hand, and no leisure for a charge which was a bore. This, it must be confessed, was somewhat different from Mrs Edgerley's anticipation of being "besieged for introductions" to the author of *Hope Hazlewood*. The young author looked wistfully into the brightness of the great drawing-room, with some hope of catching the eye of her patroness; but Mrs Edgerley was in the full business of "receiving," and had no eye except for the brilliant stream of arrivals. Marian began to be indignant, and kept her beautiful eyes full upon Agnes, watching her sister with eager sympathy. Never before, in all their serene and quiet lives, had they needed to be proud. For a moment the lip of Agnes curved and quivered—a momentary pang of girlish mortification passed over her face—then they both drew back suddenly to a table covered with books and portfolios, which stood behind them. They did not say a word to each other—they bent down over the prints and pictures with a sudden impulse of self-command and restraint: no one took the slightest notice of them; they stood quite alone in these magnificent rooms, which were slowly filling with strange faces. Agnes was afraid to look up, lest any one should see that there were actual tears under her eyelids. How she fancied she despised herself for such a weakness! But, after all, it was a hard enough lesson for neophytes so young and innocent,—so they stood very silent, bending closely over the picture-books, overcoming as they could their sudden mortification and disappointment. No one disturbed them in their solitary enjoyment of their little table, and for once in their life they did not say a word to each other, but bravely fought out the crisis within themselves, and rose again with all the pride of sensitive and imaginative natures to the emergency. With a sudden impulsive movement Agnes drew a chair to the table, and made Marian sit down upon it. "Now, we will suppose we are at the play," said Agnes, with youthful contempt and defiance, leaning her arm upon the back of the chair, and looking at the people instead of the picture-books. Marian was not so rapid in her change of mood—she sat still, shading her face with her hand, with a flush upon her cheek, and an angry cloud on her beautiful young brow. Yes, Marian was extremely angry. Mortification on her own account did not affect her—but that all these people, who no doubt were only rich people and nobodies—that they should neglect Agnes!—this was more than her sisterly equanimity could bear.

Agnes Atheling was not beautiful. When people looked at her, they never thought of her face, what were its features or its complexion. These were both agreeable enough to make no detraction from the interest of the bright and animated intelligence which was indeed the only beauty belonging to her. She did not know herself with what entire and transparent honesty her eyes and her lips expressed her sentiments; and it never occurred to her that her own looks, as she stood thus, somewhat defiant, and full of an imaginative and heroical pride, looking out upon all those strangers, made the brightest comment possible upon the scene. How her eye brightened with pleasure as it fell on a pleasant face—how her lip laughed when something ridiculous caught her rapid attention—how the soft lines on her forehead drew together when something displeased her delicate fancy—and how a certain natural delight in the graceful grouping and brilliant action of the scene before her lighted up all her face—was quite an unknown fact to Agnes. It was remarkable enough, however, in an assembly of people whose looks were regulated after the most approved principles, and who were generally adepts in the admirable art of expressing nothing. And then there was Marian, very cloudy, looking up under the shadow of her hand like an offended fairy queen. Though Mrs Edgerley was lost in the stream of her arriving guests, and the beautiful young chaperone she had committed them to took no notice whatever of her charge, tired eyes, which were looking out for something to interest them, gradually fixed upon Agnes and Marian. One or two observers asked who they were, but nobody could answer the question. They were quite by themselves, and evidently knew no one; and a little interest began to rise about them, which the girls, making their own silent observations upon everything, and still sometimes with a little wistfulness looking for Mrs Edgerley, had not yet begun to see.

When an old gentleman came to their table, and startled them a little by turning over the picture-books. He was an ancient beau—the daintiest of old gentlemen—with a blue coat and a white waistcoat, and the most delicate of ruffles. His hair—so much as he had—was perfectly white, and his high bald forehead, and even his face, looked like a piece of ivory curiously carved into wrinkles. He was not by any means a handsome old man, yet it was evident enough that this peculiar look and studied dress belonged to a notability, whose coat and cambric, and the great shining diamond upon whose wrinkled ashen-white hand, belonged to his character, and were part of himself. He was an old connoisseur, critic, and fine gentleman, with a collection of old china, old jewels, rare small pictures, and curious books, enough to craze the whole dilettanti world when it came to the prolonged and fabulous sale, which was its certain end. And he was a connoisseur in other things than silver and china. He was somewhat given to patronising young people; and the common judgment gave him credit for great kindness and benignity. But it was not benignity and kindness which drew Mr Agar to the side of Agnes and Marian. Personal amusement was a much more prevailing inducement than benevolence with the dainty old dilettante. They were deceived, of course, as youth is invariably; for despite the pure selfishness of the intention, the effect, as it happened, was kind.

Mr Agar began a conversation by remarking upon the books, and drew forth a shy reply from both; then he managed gradually to change his position, and to survey the assembled company along with them, but with his most benign and patriarchal expression. He was curious to hear in words those comments which Agnes constantly made with her eyes; and he was pleased to observe the beauty of the younger sister—the perfect unconscious grace of all her movements and attitudes. They thought they had found the most gracious of friends, these simple girls; they had not the remotest idea that he was only a connoisseur.

"Then you do not know many of those people?" said Mr Agar, following Agnes's rapid glances. "Ah, old Lady Knightly! is that a friend of yours?"

"No; I was thinking of the old story of 'Thank you for your Diamonds,'" said Agnes, who could not help drawing back a little, and casting down her eyes for the moment, while the sound of her own voice, low as it was, brought a sudden flush to her cheek. "I did not think diamonds had been so pretty; they look as if they were alive."

"Ah, the diamonds!" said the old critic, looking at the unconscious object of Agnes's observation, who was an old lady, wrinkled and gorgeous, with a leaping, twinkling band of light circling her time-shrivelled brow. "Yes, she looks as if she had dressed for a masquerade in the character of Night—eh? Poor old lady, with her lamps of diamonds! Beauty, you perceive, does not need so many tapers to show its whereabouts."

"But there are a great many beautiful people here," said Agnes, "and a great many jewels. I think, sir, it is kind of people to wear them, because all the pleasure is to us who look on."

"You think so? Ah, then beauty itself, I suppose, is pure generosity, and *we* have all the pleasure of it," said the amused old gentleman; "that is comfortable doctrine, is it not?" And he looked at Marian, who glanced up blushingly, yet with a certain pleasure. He smiled, yet he looked benignant and fatherly; and this was an extremely agreeable view of the matter, and made it much less embarrassing to acknowledge oneself pretty. Marian felt herself indebted to this kind old man.

"And you know no one—not even Mrs Edgerley, I presume?" said the old gentleman. They both interrupted him in haste to correct this, but he only smiled the more, and went on. "Well, I shall be benevolent, and tell you who your neighbours are; but I cannot follow those rapid eyes. Yes, I perceive you have made a good pause for a beginning—that is our pretty hostess's right honourable papa. Poor Winterbourne! he was sadly clumsy about his business. He is one of those unfortunate men who cannot do a wicked thing without doing it coarsely. You perceive, he is stopping to speak to Lady Theodosia—dear Lady Theodosia, who writes those sweet books! Nature intended she should be merry and vulgar, and art has made her very fine, very sentimental, and full of tears. There is an unfortunate youth wandering alone behind everybody's back. That is a miserable new poet, whom Mrs Edgerley has deluded hither under the supposition that he is to be the lion of the evening. Poor fellow! he is looking demoniacal, and studying an epigram. Interested in the poet—eh?"

"Yes, sir," said Agnes, with her usual respect; "but we were thinking of ourselves, who were something the same," she added quickly; for Mr Agar had seen the sudden look which passed between the sisters.

"Something the same! then I am to understand that you are a poet?" said the old gentleman, with his unvarying benignity. "No!—what then? A musician? No; an artist? Come, you puzzle me. I shall begin to suppose you have written a novel if you do not explain."

The animated face of Agnes grew blank in a moment; she drew farther back, and blushed painfully. Marian immediately drew herself up and stood upon the defensive. "Is it anything wrong to write a novel?" said Marian. Mr Agar turned upon her with his benignant smile.

"It is so, then?" said the old gentleman; "and I have not the least doubt it is an extremely clever novel. But hold! who comes here? Ah, an American! Now we must do our best to talk very brilliantly, for friend Jonathan loves the conversation of distinguished circles. Let me find a seat for you, and do not be angry that I am not an enthusiast in literary matters. We have all our hobbies, and that does not happen to be mine."

Agnes sat down passively on the chair he brought for her. The poor girl felt grievously ashamed of herself. After all, what was that poor little book, that she should ground such mighty claims upon it? Who cared for the author of *Hope Hazlewood*? Mr Agar, though he was so kind, did not even care to inquire what book it was, nor showed the smallest curiosity about its name. Agnes was so much cast down that she scarcely noticed the upright figure approaching towards them, carrying an abstracted head high in the air, and very like to run over smaller people; but Mr Agar stepped aside, and Marian touched her sister's arm. "It is Mr Endicott—look, Agnes!" whispered Marian. Both of them were stirred with sudden pleasure at sight of him; it was a known face in this dazzling wilderness, though it was not a very comely one. Mr Endicott was as much startled as themselves when glancing downward from his lofty altitude, his eye fell upon the beautiful face which had made sunshine even in the shady place of that Yankee young gentleman's self-admiring breast. The sudden discovery brightened his lofty languor for a moment. He hastened to shake hands with them, so impressively that the pretty lady and her cloud of admirers paused in their flutter of satire and compliment to look on.

"This is a pleasure I was not prepared for," said Mr Endicott. "I remember that Mr Atheling had an early acquaintance with Viscount Winterbourne—I presume an old hereditary friendship. I am rejoiced to find that such things are, even in this land of sophistication. This is a brilliant scene!"

"Indeed I do not think papa knows Lord Winterbourne," said Agnes hastily; but her low voice did not reach the ears which had been so far enlightened by Mr Endicott. "Hereditary friendship—old connections of the family; no doubt daughters of some squire in Banburyshire," said their beautiful neighbour, in a half-offended tone, to one of her especial retainers, who showed strong symptoms of desertion, and had already half-a-dozen times asked Marian's name. Unfortunate Mr Endicott! he gained a formidable rival by these ill-advised words.

"I find little to complain of generally in the most distinguished circles of your country," said Mr Endicott. "Your own men of genius may be neglected, but a foreigner of distinction always finds a welcome. This is true wisdom—for by this means we are enabled to carry a good report to the world."

"I say, what nice accounts these French fellows give of us!" burst in suddenly a very young man, who stood under the shadow of Mr Endicott. The youth who hazarded this brilliant remark did not address anybody in particular, and was somewhat overpowered by the unexpected honour of an answer from Mr Agar.

"Trench journalists, and newspaper writers of any country, are of course the very best judges of manners and morals," said the old gentleman, with a smile; "the other three estates are more than usually fallible; the fourth is the nearest approach to perfection which we can find in man."

"Sir," said Mr Endicott, "in my country we can do without Queen, Lords, and Commons; but we cannot do without the Press—that is, the exponent of every man's mind and character, the legitimate vehicle of instructive experiences. The Press, sir, is Progress—the only effective agency ever invented for the perfection of the human race."

"Oh, I am sure I quite agree with you. I am quite in love with the newspapers; they do make one so delightfully out of humour," said Mrs Edgerley, suddenly making her appearance; "and really, you know, when they speak of society, it is quite charming—so absurd! Sir Langham Portland—Miss Atheling. I have been so longing to come to you. Oh, and you must know Mr Agar. Mr Agar, I want to introduce you to my charming young friend, the author of *Hope Hazlewood*; is it not wonderful? I was sure you, who are so fond of people of genius, would be pleased to know her. And there is dear Lady Theodosia, but she is so surrounded. You must come to the Willows—you must indeed; I positively insist upon it. For what can one do in an evening? and so many of my friends want to know you. We go down in a fortnight. I shall certainly calculate upon you. Oh, I never take a refusal; it was *so* kind of you to come to-night."

Before she had ceased speaking, Mrs Edgerley was at the other end of the room, conversing with some one else, by her pretty gestures. Sir Langham Portland drew himself up like a guardsman, as he was, on the other side of Marian, and made original remarks about the picture-books, somewhat to the amusement, but more to the dismay of the young beauty, unaccustomed to such distinguished attentions. Mr Agar occupied himself with Agnes; he told her all about the Willows, Mrs Edgerley's pretty house at Richmond, which was always amusing, said the old gentleman. He was very pleasantly amused himself with Agnes's bright respondent face, which, however, this wicked old critic was fully better pleased with while its mortification and disappointment lasted. Mr Endicott remained standing in front of the group, watching the splendid guardsman with a misanthropic eye. This, however, was not very amusing; and the enlightened American gracefully took from his pocket the daintiest of pocket-books, fragrant with Russia leather and clasped with gold. From this delicate enclosure Mr Endicott selected with care a letter and a card, and, armed with these formidable implements, turned round upon the unconscious old gentleman. When Mr Agar caught a glimpse of this impending assault, his momentary look of dismay would have delighted himself, could he have seen it. "I have the honour of bearing a letter of introduction," said Mr Endicott, closing upon the unfortunate connoisseur, and thrusting before his eyes the weapons of offence—the moral bowie-knife and revolver, which were the weapons of this young gentleman's warfare. Mr Agar looked his assailant in the face, but did not put forth his hand.

"At my own house," said the ancient beau, with a gracious smile: "who could be stoic enough to do justice to the most distinguished of strangers, under such irresistible distractions as I find here?"

Poor Mr Endicott! He did not venture to be offended, but he was extinguished notwithstanding, and could not make head against his double disappointment; for there stood the guardsman speaking through his mustache of Books of Beauty, and holding his place like the most faithful of sentinels by Marian Atheling's side.

CHAPTER XXVIII
A FOE

"I shall have to relinquish my charge of you," said the young chaperone, for the first time addressing Agnes. Agnes started immediately, and rose.

"It is time for us to go," she said with eager shyness, "but I did not like. May we follow you? If it would not trouble you, it would be a great kindness, for we know no one here."

"Why did you come, then?" said the lady. Agnes's ideas of politeness were sorely tried to-night.

"Indeed," said the young author, with a sudden blush and courage, "I cannot tell why, unless because Mrs Edgerley asked us; but I am sure it was very foolish, and we will know better another time."

"Yes, it is always tiresome, unless one knows everybody," said the pretty young matron, slowly rising, and accepting with a careless grace the arm which somebody offered her. The girls rose hastily to follow. Mr Agar had left them some time before, and even the magnificent guardsman had been drawn away from his sentryship. With a little tremor, looking at nobody, and following very close in the steps of their leader, they glided along through the brilliant groups of the great drawing-room. But, alas! they were not fated to reach the door in unobserved safety. Mr Endicott, though he was improving his opportunities, though he had already fired another letter of introduction at somebody else's head, and listened to his heart's content to various snatches of that most brilliant and wise conversation going on everywhere around him, had still kept up a distant and lofty observation of the lady of his love. He hastened forward to them now, as with beating hearts they pursued their way, keeping steadily behind their careless young guide. "You are going?" said Mr Endicott, making a solemn statement of the fact. "It is early; let me see you to your carriage."

But they were glad to keep close to him a minute afterwards, while they waited for that same carriage, the Islingtonian fly, with Charlie in it, which was slow to recognise its own name when called. Charlie rolled himself out as the vehicle drew up, and came to the door like a man to receive his sisters.

A gentleman stood by watching the whole scene with a little amusement—the shy girls, the big brother, the officious American. This was a man of singularly pale complexion, very black hair, and a face over which the skin seemed to be strained so tight that his features were almost ghastly. He was old, but he did not look like his age; and it was impossible to suppose that he ever could have looked young. His smile was not at all a pleasant smile. Though it came upon his face by his own will, he seemed to have no power of putting it off again; and it grew into a faint spasmodic sneer, offensive and repellent. Charlie looked him in the face with a sudden impulse of pugnacity—he looked at Charlie with this bloodless and immovable smile. The lad positively lingered, though his fly "stopped the way," to bestow another glance upon this remarkable personage, and their eyes met in a full and mutual stare. Whether either person, the old man or the youth, were moved by a thrill of presentiment, we are not able to say; but there was little fear hereafter of any want of mutual recognition. Despite the world of social distinction, age, and power which lay between them, Charlie Atheling looked at Lord Winterbourne, and Lord Winterbourne looked at Charlie. It was their first point of contact; neither of them could read the fierce mutual conflict, the ruin, despair, and disgrace which lay in the future, in that first look of impulsive hostility; but as the great man entered his carriage, and the boy plunged into the fly, their thoughts for the moment were full of each other—so full that neither could understand the sudden distinct recognition of this first touch of fate.

"No; mamma was quite right," said Agnes; "we cannot be great friends nor very happy with people so different from ourselves."

And the girls sighed. They were pleased, yet they were disappointed. It was impossible to deny that the reality was as far different from the imagination as anything could be; and really nobody had been in the smallest degree concerned about the author of *Hope Hazlewood*. Even Marian was compelled to acknowledge that.

"But then," cried this eager young apologist, "they were not literary people; they were not good judges; they were common people, like what you might see anywhere, though they might be great ladies and fine gentlemen; it was easy to see *we* were not very great, and they did not understand *you*."

"Hush," said Agnes quickly; "they were rather kind, I think—especially Mr Agar; but they did not care at all for us: and why should they, after all?"

"So it was a failure," said Charlie. "I say, who was that man—that fellow at the door?"

"Oh, Charlie, you dreadful boy! that was Lord Winterbourne," cried Marian. "Mr Agar told us who he was."

"Who's Mr Agar?" asked Charlie. "And so that's him—that's the man that will take the Old Wood Lodge! I wish he would. I knew I owed him something. I'd like to see him try!"

"And Mrs Edgerley is his daughter," said Agnes. "Is it not strange? And I suppose we shall all be neighbours in the country. But Mr Endicott said quite loud, so that everybody could hear, that papa was a friend of Lord Winterbourne's. I do not like people to slight us; but I don't like to deceive them either. There was *that* gentleman—that Sir Langham. I suppose he thought *we* were great people, Marian, like the rest of the people there."

In the darkness Marian pouted, frowned, and laughed within herself. "I don't think it matters much what Sir Langham thought," said Marian; for already the young beauty began to feel her "greatness," and smiled at her own power.

CHAPTER XXIX
FAMILY SENTIMENTS

When the fly jumbled into Bellevue, the lighted window, which always illuminated the little street, shone brighter than ever in the profound darkness of this late night, when all the respectable inhabitants for more than an hour had been asleep. Papa and Mamma, somewhat drowsily, yet with a capacity for immediate waking-up only to be felt under these circumstances, had unanimously determined to sit up for the girls; and the window remained bright, and the inmates wakeful, for a full hour after the rumbling "fly," raising all the dormant echoes of the neighbourhood, had rolled off to its nightly shelter. The father and the mother listened with the most perfect patience to the detail of everything, excited in spite of themselves by their children's companionship with "the great," yet considerably resenting, and much disappointed by the failure of those grand visions, in which all night the parental imagination had pictured to itself an admiring assembly hanging upon the looks of those innocent and simple girls. Mr and Mrs Atheling on this occasion were somewhat disposed, we confess, to make out a case of jealousy and malice against the fashionable guests of Mrs Edgerley. It was always the way, Papa said. They always tried to keep everybody down, and treated aspirants superciliously; and in the climax of his indignation, under his breath, he added something about those "spurns which patient merit of the unworthy takes." Mrs Atheling did not quote Shakespeare, but she was quite as much convinced that it was their "rank in life" which had prevented Agnes and Marian from taking a sovereign place in the gay assembly they had just left. The girls themselves gave no distinct judgment on the subject; but now that the first edge of her mortification had worn off, Agnes began to have great doubts upon this matter. "We had no claim upon them—not the least," said Agnes; "they never saw us before; we were perfect strangers; why should they trouble themselves about us, simply because I had written a book?"

"Do not speak nonsense, my dear—do not tell me," said Mrs Atheling, with agitation: "they had only to use their own eyes and see—as if they often had such an opportunity! My dear, I know better; you need not speak to me!"

"And everybody has read your book, Agnes—and no doubt there are scores of people who would give anything to know you," said Papa with dignity. "The author of *Hope Hazlewood* is a different person from Agnes Atheling. No, no—it is not that they don't know your proper place; but they keep everybody down as long as they can. Now, mind, one day you will turn the tables upon them; I am very sure of that."

Agnes said no more, but went up to her little white room completely unconvinced upon the subject. Miss Willsie saw the tell-tale light in this little high window in the middle of the night—when it was nearly daylight, the old lady said—throwing a friendly gleam upon the two young controversialists as they debated this difficult question. Agnes, of course, with all the heat of youth and innovation, took the extreme side of the question. "It is easy enough to write—any one can write," said the young author, triumphant in her argument, yet in truth somewhat mortified by her triumph. "But even if it was not, there are greater things in this world than books, and almost all other books are greater than novels; and I do think it was the most foolish thing in the world to suppose that clever people like these—for they were all clever people—would take any notice of me."

To which arguments, all and several, Marian returned only a direct, unhesitating, and broad negative. It was *not* easy to write, and there were *not* greater things than books, and it was not at all foolish to expect a hundred times more than ever their hopes had expected. "It is very wrong of you to say so, Agnes," said Marian. "Papa is quite right; it will all be as different as possible by-and-by; and if you have nothing more sensible to say than that, I shall go to sleep."

Saying which, Marian turned round upon her pillow, virtuously resisted all further temptations, and closed her beautiful eyes upon the faint grey dawn which began to steal in between the white curtains. They thought their minds were far too full to go to sleep. Innocent imaginations! five minutes after, they were in the very sweetest enchanted country of the true fairyland of dreams.

While Charlie, in his sleep in the next room, laboriously struggled all night with a bloodless apparition, which smiled at him from an open doorway—fiercely fought and struggled against it—mastered it—got it down, but only to begin once more the tantalising combat. When he rose in the morning, early as usual, the youth set his teeth at the recollection, and with an attempt to give a reason for this instinctive enmity, fiercely hoped that Lord Winterbourne would try to take from his father his little inheritance. Charlie, who was by no means of a metaphysical turn, did not trouble himself at all to inquire into the grounds of his own unusual pugnacity. He "knew he owed him something," and though my Lord Winterbourne was a viscount and an ex-minister, and Charlie only a poor man's son and a copying-clerk, he fronted the great man's image with indomitable confidence, and had no more doubt of his own prowess than of his entire goodwill in the matter. He did not think very much more of his opponent in this case than he did of the big folios in the office, and had as entire confidence in his own ability to bring the enemy down.

But it was something of a restless night to Papa and Mamma. They too talked in their darkened chamber, too proper and too economical to waste candlelight upon subjects so unprofitable, of old events and people half forgotten;—how the first patroness of Agnes should be the daughter of the man between whom and themselves there existed some unexplained connection of old friendship or old enmity, or both;—how circumstances beyond their guidance conspired to throw them once more in the way of persons and plans which they had heard nothing of for more than twenty years. These things were very strange and troublous events to Mr Atheling and his wife. The past, which nearer grief and closer pleasure—all their family life, full as that was of joy and sorrow—had thrown so far away and out of remembrance, came suddenly back before them in all the clearness of youthful recollection. Old feelings returned strong and fresh into their minds. They went back, and took up the thread of this history, whatever it might be, where they had dropped it twenty years ago; and with a thrill of deeper interest, wondered and inquired how this influence would affect their children. To themselves now little could happen; their old friend or their old enemy could do neither harm nor benefit to their accomplished lives—but the children!—the children, every one so young, so hopeful, and so well endowed; all so strangely brought into sudden contact, at a double point, with this one sole individual, who had power to disturb the rest of the father and the mother. They relapsed into silence suddenly, and were quieted by the thought.

"It is not our doing—it is not our seeking," said Mr Atheling at length. "If the play wants a last act, Mary, it will not be your planning nor mine; and as for the children, they are in the hands of God."

So in the grey imperfect dawn which lightened on the faces of the sleeping girls, whose sweet youthful rest was far too deep to be broken even by the growing light, these elder people closed their eyes, not to sleep, but to pray. If evil were about to come—if danger were lurking in the air around them—they had this only defence against it. It was not the simple faith of youth which dictated these prayers; it was a deeper and a closer urgency, which cried aloud and would not cease, but yet was solemn with the remembrance of times when God's pleasure was not to grant them their petitions. The young ones slept in peace, but with fights and triumphs manifold in their young dreams. The father and the mother held a vigil for them, holding up holy hands for their defence and safety; and so the morning came at last, brightly, to hearts which feared no evil, or when they feared, put their apprehensions at once into the hand of God.

CHAPTER XXX
AGNES'S FORTUNE

The morning, like a good fairy, came kindly to these good people, increasing in the remembrance of the girls the impression of pleasure, and lessening that of disappointment. They came, after all, to be very well satisfied with their reception at Mrs Edgerley's. And now her second and most important invitation remained to be discussed—the Willows— the pretty house at Richmond, with the river running sweetly under the shadow of its trees; the company, which was sure to include, as Mr Agar said, *some* people worth knowing, and which that ancient connoisseur himself did not refuse to join. Agnes and Marian looked with eager eyes on the troubled brow of Mamma; a beautiful vision of the lawn and the river, flowers and sunshine, the sweet silence of "the country," and the unfamiliar music of running water and rustling trees, possessed the young imaginations for the time to the total disregard of all sublunary considerations. *They* did not think for a moment of Lord Winterbourne's daughter, and the strange chance which could make them inmates of her house; for Lord Winterbourne himself was not a person of any importance in the estimation of the girls. But more than that, they did not even think of their wardrobe, important as that consideration was; they did not recollect how entirely unprovided they were for such a visit, nor how the family finances, strait and unelastic, could not possibly stretch to so new and great an expenditure. But all these things, which brought no cloud upon Agnes and Marian, conspired to embarrass the brow of the family mother. She thought at the same moment of Lord Winterbourne and of the brown merinos; of this strange acquaintanceship, mysterious and full of fate as it seemed; and of the little black silk cloaks which were out of fashion, and the bonnets with the faded ribbons. It was hard to deny the girls so great a pleasure; but how could it be done?

And for a day or two following the household remained in great uncertainty upon this point, and held every evening, on the engrossing subject of ways and means, a committee of the whole house. This, however, we are grieved to say, was somewhat of an unprofitable proceeding; for the best advice which Papa could give on so important a subject was, that the girls must of course have everything proper if they went. "If they went!—

that is exactly the question," said the provoked and impatient ruler of all. "But are they to go? and how are we to get everything proper for them?" To these difficult questions Mr Atheling attempted no answer. He was a wise man, and knew his own department, and prudently declined any interference in the legitimate domain of the other head of the house.

Mrs Atheling was by no means addicted to disclosing the private matters of her own family life, yet she carried this important question through the faded wallflowers to crave the counsel of Miss Willsie. Miss Willsie was not at all pleased to have such a matter submitted to her. *Her* supreme satisfaction would have lain in criticising, finding fault, and helping on. Now reduced to the painful alternative of giving an opinion, the old lady pronounced a vague one in general terms, to the effect that if there was one thing she hated, it was to see poor folk striving for the company of them that were in a different rank in life; but whenever this speech was made, and her conscience cleared, Miss Willsie began to inquire zealously what "the silly things had," and what they wanted, and set about a mental turning over of her own wardrobe, where were a great many things which she had worn in her own young days, and which were "none the worse," as she said— but they were not altogether adapted for the locality of the Willows. Miss Willsie turned them over not only in her own mind, but in her own parlour, where her next visitor found her as busy with her needle and her shears as any cottar matron ever was, and anxiously bent on the same endeavour to "make auld things look amaist as weel's the new." It cost Miss Willsie an immense deal of trouble, but it was not half so successful a business as the repairs of that immortal Saturday Night.

But the natural course of events, which had cleared their path for them many times before, came in once more to make matters easy. Mr Burlington, of whom nothing had been heard since the day of that eventful visit to his place—Mr Burlington, who since then had brought out a second edition of *Hope Hazlewood*, announced himself ready to "make a proposal" for the book. Now, there had been many and great speculations in the house on this subject of "Agnes's fortune." They were as good at the magnificent arithmetic of fancy as Major Pendennis was, and we will not say that, like him, they had not leaped to their thousands a-year. They had all, however, been rather prudent in committing themselves to a sum—nobody would guess positively what it was to be—but some indefinite and fabulous amount, a real fortune, floated in the minds of all: to the father and mother a substantial provision for Agnes, to the girls an inexhaustible fund of pleasure, comfort, and charity. The proposal came—it was not a fabulous and magnificent fortune, for the author of *Hope Hazlewood* was only Agnes Atheling, and not Arthur Pendennis. For the first moment, we are compelled to confess, they looked at each other with blank faces, entirely cast down and disappointed: it was not an inexhaustible fairy treasure—it was only a hundred and fifty pounds.

Yes, most tender-hearted reader! these were not the golden days of Sir Walter, nor was this young author a literary Joan of Arc. She got her fortune in a homely fashion like other people—at first was grievously disappointed about it—formed pugnacious resolutions, and listened to all the evil stories of the publishing ghouls with satisfaction and indignant faith. But by-and-by this angry mood softened down; by-and-by the real glory of such an unrealisable heap of money began to break upon the girls. A hundred and fifty pounds, and nothing to do with it—no arrears to pay—nothing to make up—can any one suppose a position of more perfect felicity? They came to see it bit by bit dawning upon them in gradual splendour—content blossomed into satisfaction, satisfaction unfolded into delight. And then to think of laying by such a small sum would be foolish, as the girls reasoned; so its very insignificance increased the pleasure. It was not a dull treasure, laid up in a bank, or "invested," as Papa had solemnly proposed to invest "Agnes's fortune;" it was a delightful little living stream of abundance, already in imagination overflowing and brightening everything. It would buy Mamma the most magnificent of brocades, and Bell and Beau such frocks as never were seen before out of fairyland. It would take them all to the Old Wood Lodge, or even to the seaside; it would light up with books and pictures, and pretty things, the respectable family face of Number Ten, Bellevue. There was no possibility of exhausting the capacities of this marvellous sum of money, which, had it been three or four times as much, as the girls discovered, could not have been half as good for present purposes. The delight of spending money was altogether new to them: they threw themselves into it with the most gleeful abandonment (in imagination), and threw away their fortune royally, and with genuine enjoyment in the process; and very few millionaires have ever found as much pleasure in the calculation of their treasures as Agnes and Marian Atheling, deciding over and over again how they were to spend it, found in this hundred and fifty pounds.

In the mean time, however, Papa carried it off to the office, and locked it up there for security—for they all felt that it would not be right to trust to the commonplace defences of Bellevue with such a prodigious sum of money in the house.

CHAPTER XXXI
EXTRAVAGANCE

It was a July day, brilliant and dazzling; the deep-blue summer sky arched over these quiet houses, a very heaven of sunshine and calm; the very leaves were golden in the flood of light, and grateful shadows fell from the close walls, and a pleasant summer fragrance came from within the little enclosures of Bellevue. Nothing was stirring in the silent little suburban street—the very sounds came slow and soft through the luxurious noonday air, into which now and then blew the little capricious breath of a cool breeze, like some invisible fairy fan making a current in the golden atmosphere. Safe under the shelter of green blinds and opened windows, the feminine population reposed in summer indolence, mistresses too languid to scold, and maids to be improved by the same. In the day, the other half of mankind, all mercantile and devoted to business, deserted Bellevue and perhaps were not less drowsy in their several offices, where dust had to answer all the purpose of those trim venetian defences, than their wives and daughters were at home.

But before the door of Number Ten stood a vehicle—let no one scorn its unquestioned respectability,—it was The Fly. The fly was drawn by an old white horse, of that bony and angular development peculiar to this rank of professional eminence. This illustrious animal gave character and distinction at once to the equipage. The smartest and newest brougham in existence, with such a steed attached to it, must at once have taken rank, in the estimation of all beholders, as a true and unmistakable Fly. The coachman was in character; he had a long white livery-coat, and a hat very shiny, and bearing traces of various indentations. As he sat upon his box in the sunshine, he nodded in harmony with the languid branches of the lilac-bushes. Though he was not averse to a job, he marvelled much how anybody who could stay at home went abroad under this burning sun, or troubled themselves with occupations. So too thought the old white horse, switching his old white tail in vain pursuit of the summer flies which troubled him; and so even thought Hannah, Miss Willsie's pretty maid, as she looked out from the gate of Killiecrankie Lodge, shading her eyes with her hand, marvelling, half in envy, half in pity, how any one could think even of "pleasuring" on such a day.

With far different sentiments from these languid and indolent observers, the Athelings prepared for their unusual expedition. Firmly compressed into Mrs Atheling's purse were five ten-pound notes, crisp and new, and the girls, with a slight tremor of terror enhancing their delight, had secretly vowed that Mamma should not be permitted to bring anything in the shape of money home. They were going to spend fifty pounds. That was their special mission—and when you consider that very rarely before had they helped at the spending of more than fifty shillings, you may fancy the excitement and delight of this family enterprise. They had calculated beforehand what everything was to cost—they had left a margin for possibilities—they had all their different items written down on a very long piece of paper, and now the young ladies were dancing Bell and Beau through the garden, and waiting for Mamma.

For the twin babies were to form part of this most happy party. Bell and Beau were to have an ecstatic drive in that most delightful of carriages which the two big children and the two little ones at present stood regarding with the sincerest admiration. If Agnes had any doubt at all about the fly, it was a momentary fear lest somebody should suppose it to be their own carriage—a contingency not at all probable. In every other view of the question, the fly was scarcely second even to Mrs Edgerley's sublime and stately equipage; and it is quite impossible to describe the rapture with which this magnificent vehicle was contemplated by Bell and Beau.

At last Mamma came down stairs in somewhat of a flutter, and by no means satisfied that she was doing right in thus giving in to the girls. Mrs Atheling still, in spite of all their persuasions, could not help thinking it something very near a sin to spend wilfully, and at one doing, so extraordinary a sum as fifty pounds—"a quarter's income!" she said solemnly. But Papa was very nearly as foolish on the subject as Agnes and Marian, and the good mother could not make head against them all. She was alarmed at this first outbreak of "awful" extravagance, but she could not quite refuse to be pleased either with the pleasant piece of business, with the delight of the girls, and the rapture of the babies, nor to feel the glory in her own person of "shopping" on so grand a scale—

"My sister and my sister's child,
Myself and children three."

The fly was not quite so closely packed as the chaise of Mrs Gilpin, yet it was very nearly as full as that renowned conveyance. They managed to get in "five precious souls," and the white horse languidly set out upon his journey, and the coachman, only half awake, still nodded on his box. Where they went to, we will not betray their confidence by telling. It was an erratic course, and included all manner of shops and purchases. Before they had got nearly to the end of their list, they were quite fatigued with their labours, and found it rather cumbrous, after all, to choose the shops they wanted from the "carriage" windows, a splendid but inconvenient necessity. Then Bell and Beau grew very tired, wanted to go home, and were scarcely to be solaced even with cakes innumerable. Perfect and unmixed delights are not to be found under the sun; and though the fly went back to Bellevue laden with parcels beyond the power of arithmetic; though the girls had accomplished their wicked will, and the purse of Mrs Atheling had shrunk into the ghost of its former size, yet the accomplished errand was not half so delightful as were those exuberant and happy intentions, which could now be talked over no more. They all grew somewhat silent, as they drove home—"vanity of vanities—" Mrs Atheling and her daughters were in a highly reflective state of mind, and rather given to moralising; while extremely wearied, sleepy, and uncomfortable were poor little Bell and Beau.

But at last they reached home—at last the pleasant sight of Susan, and the fragrance of the tea, which, as it was now pretty late in the afternoon, Susan had prepared to refresh them, restored their flagging spirits. They began to open out their parcels, and fight their battles over again. They examined once more, outside and inside, the pretty little watches which Papa had insisted on as the first of all their purchases. Papa thought a watch was a most important matter—the money spent in such a valuable piece of property was *invested*; and Mrs Atheling herself, as she took her cup of tea, looked at these new acquisitions with extreme pride, good pleasure, and a sense of importance. They had put their bonnets on the sofa—the table overflowed with rolls of silk and pieces of ribbon half unfolded; Bell and Beau, upon the hearth-rug, played with the newest noisiest toys which could be found for them; and even Susan, when she came to ask if her mistress would take another cup, secretly confessed within herself that there never was such a littered and untidy room.

When there suddenly came a dash and roll of rapid wheels, ringing into all the echoes. Suddenly, with a gleam and bound, a splendid apparition crossed the window, and two magnificent bay-horses drove up before the little gate. Her very watch, new and well-beloved, almost fell from the fingers of Agnes. They looked at each other with blank faces—they listened in horror to the charge of artillery immediately discharged upon their door—nobody had self-possession to apprehend Susan on the way, and exhort her to remember the best room. And Susan, greatly fluttered, forgot the sole use of this sacred apartment. They all stood dismayed, deeply sensible of the tea upon the table, and the extraordinary confusion of the room, when suddenly into the midst of them, radiant and splendid, floated Mrs Edgerley—Mayfair come to visit Bellevue.

CHAPTER XXXII
A GREAT VISITOR

Mayfair came in, radiant, blooming, splendid, with a rustle of silks, a flutter of feathers, an air of fragrance, like a fairy creature not to be molested by the ruder touches of fortune or the world. Bellevue stood up to receive her in the person of Mrs Atheling, attired in a black silk gown which had seen service, and hastily setting down a cup of tea from her hand. The girls stood between the two, an intermediate world, anxious and yet afraid to interpret between them; for Marian's beautiful hair had fallen down upon her white neck, and Agnes's collar had been pulled awry, and her pretty muslin dress sadly crushed and broken by the violent hands of Bell and Beau. The very floor on which Mrs Edgerley's pretty foot pressed the much-worn carpet, was strewed with little frocks for those unruly little people. The sofa was occupied by three bonnets, and Mamma's new dress hung over the back of the easy-chair. You may laugh at this account of it, but Mamma, and Marian, and Agnes were a great deal more disposed to cry at the reality. To think that, of all days in the world, this great lady should have chosen to come to-day!

"Now, pray don't let me disturb anything. Oh, I am so delighted to find you quite at home! It is quite kind of you to let me come in," cried Mrs Edgerley—"and indeed you need not introduce me. When one has read *Hope Hazlewood*, one knows your mamma. Oh, that charming, delightful book! Now, confess you are quite proud of her. I am sure you must be."

"She is a very good girl," said Mrs Atheling doubtfully, flattered, but not entirely pleased—"and we are very deeply obliged to Mrs Edgerley for the kindness she has shown to our girls."

"Oh, I have been quite delighted," said Mayfair; "but pray don't speak in the third person. How charmingly fragrant your tea is!—may I have some? How delightful it must be to be able to keep rational hours. What lovely children! What beautiful darlings! Are they really yours?"

"My youngest babies," said Bellevue, somewhat stiffly, yet a little moved by the question. "We have just come in, and were fatigued. Agnes, my dear!"

But Agnes was already gone, seizing the opportunity to amend her collar, while Marian put away the bonnets, and cleared the parcels from the feet of Mrs Edgerley. With this pretty figure half-bending before her, and the other graceful cup-bearer offering her the homely refreshment she had asked for, Mrs Edgerley, though quite aware of it, did not think half so much as Mrs Atheling did about their "rank in life." The great lady was not at all nervous on this subject, but was most pleasantly and meritoriously conscious, as she took her cup of tea from the hand of Agnes, that by so doing she set them all "at their ease."

"And pray, do tell me now," said Mrs Edgerley, "how you manage in this quarter, so far from everything? It is quite delightful, half as good as a desolate island—such a pretty, quiet place! You must come to the Willows—I have quite made up my mind and settled it: indeed, you must come—so many people are dying to know you. And I must have your mamma know," said the pretty flutterer, turning round to Mrs Atheling with that air of irresistible caprice and fascinating despotism which was the most amazing thing in the world to the family mother, "that no one ever resists me: I am always obeyed, I assure you. Oh, you *must* come; I consider it quite a settled thing. Town gets so tiresome just at this time—don't you think so? I always long for the Willows—for it is really the sweetest place, and in the country one cares so much more for one's home."

"You are very kind," said Mrs Atheling, not knowing what other answer to make, and innocently supposing that her visitor had paused for a reply.

"Oh, I assure you, nothing of the kind—perfectly selfish, on the contrary," said Mrs Edgerley, with a sweet smile. "I shall be so charmed with the society of my young friends. I quite forgot to ask if you were musical. We have the greatest little genius in the world at the Willows. Such a voice!—it is a shame to hide such a gift in a drawing-room. She is—a sort of connection—of papa's family. I say it is very good of him to acknowledge her even so far, for people seldom like to remember their follies; but of course the poor child has no position, and I have even been blamed for having her in my house. She is quite a genius—wonderful: she ought to be a singer—it is quite her duty—but such a shy foolish young creature, and not to be persuaded. What charming tea! I am quite refreshed, I assure you. Oh, pray, do not disturb anything. I am so pleased you have let me come when you were *quite* at home. Now, Tuesday, remember! We shall have a delightful little party. I know you will quite enjoy it. Good-by, little darlings. On Tuesday, my love; you must on no account forget the day."

"But I am afraid they will only be a trouble—and they are not used to society," said Mrs Atheling, rising hastily before her visitor should have quite flown away; "they have never been away from home. Excuse me—I am afraid——"

"Oh, I assure you, nobody ever resists me," cried Mrs Edgerley, interrupting this speech; "I never hear such a naughty word as No. It is not possible—you cannot conceive how it would affect me; I should break my heart! It is quite decided—oh, positively it is—Tuesday—I shall so look forward to it! And a charming little party we shall be—not too many, and *so* congenial! I shall quite long for the day."

Saying which, Mrs Edgerley took her departure, keeping up her stream of talk while they all attended her to the door, and suffering no interruption. Mrs Atheling was by no means accustomed to so dashing and sudden an assault. She began slowly to bring up her reasons for declining the invitation as the carriage rolled away, carrying with it her tacit consent. She was quite at a loss to believe that this visit was real, as she returned into the encumbered parlour—such haste, patronage, and absoluteness were entirely out of Mrs Atheling's way.

"I have no doubt she is very kind," said the good mother, puzzled and much doubting; "but I am not at all sure that I approve of her—indeed, I think I would much rather you did not go."

"But she will expect us, mamma," said Agnes.

That was unquestionable. Mrs Atheling sat very silent all the remainder of the day, pondering much upon this rapid and sudden visitation, and blaming herself greatly for her want of readiness. And then the "poor child" who had no position, and whose duty it was to be a singer, was she a proper person to breathe the same air as Agnes and Marian? Bellevue was straiter in its ideas than Mayfair. The mother reflected with great self-reproach and painful doubts; for the girls were so pleased with the prospect, and it was so hard to deny them the expected pleasure. Mrs Atheling at last resigned herself with a sigh. "If you must go, I expect you to take great care whom you associate with," said Mrs Atheling, very pointedly; and she sent off their new purchases up-stairs, and gave her whole attention, with a certain energy and impatience, to the clearing of the room. This had not been by any means a satisfactory day.

CHAPTER XXXIII
GOING FROM HOME

"My dear children," said Mrs Atheling solemnly, "you have never been from home before."

Suddenly arrested by the solemnity of this preamble, the girls paused—they were just going up-stairs to their own room on the last evening before setting out for the Willows. Marian's pretty arms were full of a collection of pretty things, white as the great apron with which Susan had girded her. Agnes carried her blotting-book, two or three other favourite volumes, and a candle. They stood in their pretty sisterly conjunction, almost leaning upon each other, waiting with youthful reverence for the address which Mamma was about to deliver. It was true they were leaving home for the first time, and true also that the visit was one of unusual importance. They prepared to listen with great gravity and a little awe.

"My dears, I have no reason to distrust your good sense," said Mrs Atheling, "nor indeed to be afraid of you in any way—but to be in a strange house is very different from being at home. Strangers will not have the same indulgence as we have had for all your fancies—you must not expect it; and people may see that you are of a different rank in life, and perhaps may presume upon you. You must be very careful. You must not copy Mrs Edgerley, or any other lady, but *observe* what they do, and rule yourselves by it; and take great care what acquaintances you form; for even in such a house as that," said Mamma, with emphasis and dignity, suddenly remembering the "connection of the family" of whom Mrs Edgerley had spoken, "there may be some who are not fit companions for you."

"Yes, mamma," said Agnes. Marian looked down into the apronful of lace and muslin, and answered nothing. A variable blush and as variable a smile testified to a little consciousness on the part of the younger sister. Agnes for once was the more matter-of-fact of the two.

"At your time of life," continued the anxious mother, "a single day may have as much effect as many years. Indeed, Marian, my love, it is nothing to smile about. You must be very careful; and, Agnes, you are the eldest—you must watch over your sister. Oh, take care!—you do not know how much harm might be done in a single day."

"Take care of what, mamma?" said Marian, glancing up quickly, with that beautiful faint blush, and a saucy gleam in her eye. What do you suppose she saw as her beautiful eyes turned from her mother with a momentary imaginative look into the vacant space? Not the big head of Charlie, bending over the grammars, but the magnificent stature of Sir Langham Portland, drawn up in sentry fashion by her side; and at the recollection Marian's pretty lip could not refuse to smile.

"Hush, my dear!—you may easily know what I mean," said Mrs Atheling uneasily. "You must try not to be awkward or timid; but you must not forget how great a difference there is between Mrs Edgerley's friends and you."

"Nonsense, Mary," cried her husband, energetically. "No such thing, girls. Don't be afraid to let them know who you are, or who you belong to. But as for inferiority, if you yield to such a notion, you are no girls of mine! One of the Riverses! A pretty thing! *You*, at least, can tell any one who asks the question that your father is an honest man."

"But I suppose, papa, no one is likely to have any doubt upon the subject," said Agnes, with a little spirit. "It will be time enough to publish that when some one questions it; and that, I am sure, was not what mamma meant."

"No, my love, of course not," said Mamma, who was somewhat agitated. "What I meant is, that you are going to people whom we used to know—I mean, whom we know nothing of. They are great people—a great deal richer and higher in station than we are; and it is possible Papa may be brought into contact with them about the Old Wood Lodge; and you are young and inexperienced, and don't know the dangers you may be subjected to;—and, my dear children, what I have to say to you is, just to remember your duty, and read your Bibles, and take care!"

"Mamma! we are only going to Richmond—we are not going away from you," cried Marian in dismay.

"My dears," said Mrs Atheling, putting her handkerchief to her eyes, "I am an old woman—I know more than you do. You cannot tell where you are going; you are going into the world."

No one spoke for the moment. The young travellers themselves looked at their mother with concern and a little solemnity. Who could tell? All the young universe of romance lay at their very feet. They might be going to their fate.

"And henceforward I know," said the good mother, rising into homely and unconscious dignity, "our life will no longer be your boundary, nor our plans all your guidance. My darlings, it is not any fault of yours; you are both as obedient as when you were babies; it is Providence, and comes to every one. You are going away from me, and both your lives may be determined before you come back again. You, Marian! it is not your fault, my love; but, oh! take care."

Under the pressure of this solemn and mysterious caution, the girls at length went up-stairs. Very gravely they entered the little white room, which was somewhat disturbed out of its usual propriety, and in respectful silence Marian began to arrange her burden. She sat down upon the white bed, with her great white apron full of snowy muslin and dainty morsels of lace, stooping her beautiful head over them, with her long bright hair falling down at one side like a golden framework to her sweet cheek. Agnes stood before her holding the candle. Both were perfectly grave, quite silent, separating the sleeves and kerchiefs and collars as if it were the most solemn work in the world.

At length suddenly Marian looked up. In an instant smiles irrestrainable threaded all the soft lines of those young faces. A momentary electric touch sent them both from perfect solemnity into saucy and conscious but subdued laughter. "Agnes! what do you suppose mamma could mean?" asked Marian; and Agnes said "Hush!" and softly closed the door, lest Mamma should hear the low and restrained overflow of those sudden sympathetic smiles. Once more the apparition of the magnificent Sir Langham gleamed somewhere in a bright corner of Marian's shining eye. These incautious girls, like all their happy kind, could not be persuaded to regard with any degree of terror or solemnity the fate that came in such a shape as this.

CHAPTER XXXIV
EVERYBODY'S FANCIES

But the young adventurers had sufficient time to speculate upon their "fate," and to make up their minds whether this journey of theirs was really a fortnight's visit to Richmond, or a solemn expedition into the world, as they drove along the pleasant summer roads on their way to the Willows. They had leisure enough, but they had not inclination; they were somewhat excited, but not at all solemnised. They thought of the unknown paradise to which they were going—of their beautiful patroness and her guests; but they never paused to inquire, as they bowled pleasantly along under the elms and chestnuts, anything at all about their fate.

"How grave every one looked," said Marian. "What are all the people afraid of? for I am sure Miss Willsie wanted us to go, though she was so cross; and poor Harry Oswald, how he looked last night!"

At this recollection Marian smiled. To tell the truth, she was at present only amused by the gradual perception dawning upon her of the unfortunate circumstances of these young gentlemen. She might never have found it out had she known only Harry Oswald; but Sir Langham Portland threw light upon the subject which Marian had scarcely guessed at before. Do you think she was grateful on that account to the handsome Guardsman? Marian's sweet face brightened all over with amused half-blushing smiles. It was impossible to tell.

"But, Marian," said Agnes, "I want to be particular about one thing. We must not deceive any one. Nobody must suppose we are great ladies. If anything *should* happen of any importance, we must be sure to tell who we are."

"That you are the author of *Hope Hazlewood*," said Marian, somewhat provokingly. "Oh! Mrs Edgerley will tell everybody that; and as for me, I am only your sister—nobody will mind me."

So they drove on under the green leaves, which grew less and less dusty as they left London in the distance, through the broad white line of road, now and then passing by orchards rich with fruit—by suburban gardens and pretty villakins of better fashion than their own; now and then catching silvery gleams of the river quivering among its low green banks, like a new-bended bow. They knew as little where they were going as what was to befall them there, and were as unapprehensive in the one case as in the other. At home the mother went about her daily business, pondering with a mother's anxiety upon all the little embarrassments and distresses which might surround them among strangers, and seeing in her motherly imagination a host of pleasant perils, half alarming, half complimentary, a crowd of admirers and adorers collected round her girls. At Messrs Cash and Ledger's, Papa brooded over his desk, thinking somewhat darkly of those innocent investigators whom he had sent forth into an old world of former connections, unfortified against the ancient grudge, if such existed, and unacquainted with the ancient story. Would anything come of this acquaintanceship? Would anything come of the new position which placed them once more directly in the way of Lord Winterbourne? Papa shook his head slowly over his daybook, as ignorant as the rest of us what might have to be written upon the fair blank of the very next page—who could tell?

Charlie meanwhile, at Mr Foggo's office, buckled on his harness this important morning with a double share of resolution. As his brow rolled down with all its furrows in a frown of defiance at the "old fellow" whom he took down from the wired bookcase, it was not the old fellow, but Lord Winterbourne, against whom Charlie bit his thumb. In the depths of his heart he wished again that this natural enemy might "only try!" to usurp possession of the Old Wood Lodge. A certain excitement possessed him regarding the visit of his sisters. Once more the youth, in his hostile imagination, beheld the pale face at the door, the bloodless and spasmodic smile. "I knew I owed him something," muttered once more the instinctive enmity; and Charlie was curious and excited to come once more in contact with this mysterious personage who had raised so active and sudden an interest in his secret thoughts.

But the two immediate actors in this social drama—the family doves of inquiry, who might bring back angry thorns instead of olive branches— the innocent sweet pioneers of the incipient strife, went on untroubled in their youthful pleasure, looking at the river and the sunshine, dreaming the fairy dreams of youth. What new life they verged and bordered—what great consequences might grow and blossom from the seedtime of to-day— how their soft white hands, heedless and unconscious, might touch the trembling strings of fate—no one of all these anxious questions ever entered the charmed enclosure of this homely carriage, where they leant back into their several corners, and sung to themselves, in unthinking sympathy with the roll and hum of the leisurely wheels, conveying them on and on to their new friends and their future life. They were content to leave all questions of the kind to a more suitable season—and so, singing, smiling, whispering (though no one was near to interrupt them), went on, on their charmed way, with their youth and their light hearts, to Armida and her enchanted garden—to the world, with its syrens and its lions—forecasting no difficulties, seeing no evil. They had no day-book to brood over like Papa. To-morrow's magnificent blank of possibility was always before them, dazzling and glorious—they went forward into it with the freshest smile and the sweetest confidence. Of all the evils and perils of this wicked world, which they had heard so much of, they knew none which they, in their happy safety, were called upon to fear.